How Did I ___ ___ ... in Windows XP

Books Available

By the same authors:

BP557	How Did I Do That ... in Windows XP*
BP550	Advanced Guide to Windows XP
BP548	Easy PC Keyboard Shortcuts*
BP546	Microsoft Works Suite 2004 explained
BP545	Paint Shop Pro 8 explained*
BP544	Microsoft Office 2003 explained
BP538	Windows XP for Beginners*
BP525	Controlling Windows XP the easy way*
BP522	Microsoft Works Suite 2002 explained
BP514	Windows XP explained*
BP513	IE 6 and Outlook Express 6 explained*
BP512	Microsoft Access 2002 explained
BP511	Microsoft Excel 2002 explained
BP510	Microsoft Word 2002 explained
BP509	Microsoft Office XP explained
BP498	Using Visual Basic
BP493	Windows Me explained*
BP491	Windows 2000 explained*
BP487	Quicken 2000 UK explained*
BP486	Using Linux the easy way*
BP465	Lotus SmartSuite Millennium explained
BP433	Your own Web site on the Internet
BP341	MS-DOS explained
BP284	Programming in QuickBASIC
BP258	Learning to Program in C

If you would like to purchase a Companion Disc for any of the listed books by the same authors, apart from the ones marked with an asterisk, containing the file/program listings which appear in them, then fill in the form at the back of the book and send it to Phil Oliver at the stipulated address.

How Did I Do That ...
in Windows XP

by

N. Kantaris
and
P.R.M. Oliver

Bernard Babani (publishing) Ltd
The Grampians
Shepherds Bush Road
London W6 7NF
England
www.babanibooks.com

Please Note

Although every care has been taken with the production of this book to ensure that any projects, designs, modifications and/or programs, etc., contained herewith, operate in a correct and safe manner and also that any components specified are normally available in Great Britain, the Publishers and Author(s) do not accept responsibility in any way for the failure (including fault in design) of any project, design, modification or program to work correctly or to cause damage to any equipment that it may be connected to or used in conjunction with, or in respect of any other damage or injury that may be so caused, nor do the Publishers accept responsibility in any way for the failure to obtain specified components.

Notice is also given that if equipment that is still under warranty is modified in any way or used or connected with home-built equipment then that warranty may be void.

© 2005 BERNARD BABANI (publishing) LTD

First Published - March 2005
Reprinted - February 2006

British Library Cataloguing in Publication Data:

A catalogue record for this book is available from the British Library

ISBN 0 85934 557 2

Cover Design by Gregor Arthur
Printed and Bound in Great Britain by Cox & Wyman Ltd, Reading

About this Book

How Did I Do That ... in Windows XP was written to help users to remember how they configured their computer in the first place. Have you ever been in the situation when something has happened (like typing a date in UK format which then displays in US style - days and months reversed)? Of course you remember someone telling you how to configure the language of your keyboard, but can't think of it right now? This book will tell you how to do just that and a lot besides. The book covers both the Professional and Home editions of Windows XP, including the latest update Service Pack 2 - see the Windows Brief History.

In this book we assume that Windows XP has been installed on your computer and is up and running. If you need information on such important topics as how to upgrade, what system preparation to make before installing Windows XP, what the hardware requirements are, or which file system to select (FAT32 or NTFS), then may we suggest you refer to our other book *Windows XP explained* (BP514) also published by Bernard Babani (publishing) Ltd.

As with all our other books, this book was written with the busy person in mind. You don't need to read many hundreds of large format pages to find out what you are looking for, when just a fewer illustrated pages can get you there very quickly!

It is hoped that with the help of this book, you will be able to configure your computer, when using Windows XP, most efficiently and productively, and that you will be able to do it in the shortest possible time.

About the Authors

Noel Kantaris graduated in Electrical Engineering at Bristol University and after spending three years in the Electronics Industry in London, took up a Tutorship in Physics at the University of Queensland. Research interests in Ionospheric Physics, led to the degrees of M.E. in Electronics and Ph.D. in Physics. On return to the UK, he took up a Post-Doctoral Research Fellowship in Radio Physics at the University of Leicester, and then a lecturing position in Engineering at the Camborne School of Mines, Cornwall, (part of Exeter University), where he was also the CSM Computing Manager. At present he is IT Director of FFC Ltd.

Phil Oliver graduated in Mining Engineering at Camborne School of Mines and has specialised in most aspects of surface mining technology, with a particular emphasis on computer related techniques. He has worked in Guyana, Canada, several Middle Eastern and Central Asian countries, South Africa and the United Kingdom, on such diverse projects as: the planning and management of bauxite, iron, gold and coal mines; rock excavation contracting in the UK; international mining equipment sales and international mine consulting. He later took up a lecturing position at Camborne School of Mines (part of Exeter University) in Surface Mining and Management. He has now retired, to spend more time writing, consulting, and developing Web sites.

Acknowledgements

We would like to thank friends and colleagues, for their helpful tips and suggestions which assisted us in the writing of this book.

Trademarks

HP and **LaserJet** are registered trademarks of Hewlett Packard Corporation.

IBM is a registered trademark of International Business Machines, Inc.

Intel is a registered trademark of Intel Corporation.

Microsoft, **MS-DOS**, **Windows**, are either registered trademarks or trademarks of Microsoft Corporation.

PostScript is a registered trademark of Adobe Systems Incorporated.

All other brand and product names used in the book are recognised as trademarks, or registered trademarks, of their respective companies.

A Brief History of Windows

The early versions of Windows ran on top of the MS-DOS (Microsoft's Disc Operating System), and as such were not very stable, were prone to crashing frequently, and had limited support for networking and none at all for multiple user accounts. However, from 1992 to the present date, Microsoft released various versions of Windows which addressed these problems. These were:

Windows for Workgroups 3.1 - 1992	Allowed the control of small networked groups of computers.
Windows for Workgroups 3.11 - Late 1993	Included 32-bit file management and more networking support.
Windows 95 - 1995	The first 32-bit operating system.
Windows 98 - 1998	It ran faster, crashed less often, and supported a host of new technologies.
Windows 98 Second Edition - Mid-1999	It put right many faults reported by users.
Windows Me - Late 2000	A direct upgrade to Windows 95/98 for the home PC. It loaded faster, ran more reliably, and, if things went radically wrong through user interference, could be made to return to a previous working version of the Operating System.

Windows 2000 Professional - Early 2000	Users of Windows 95/98 could easily upgrade to the Windows 2000.
Windows XP - Late 2001	Windows XP comes in two flavours; the Home edition as the direct upgrade to Windows 98/Me for home users and the Professional edition (with additional functionality) for Windows 2000 or business users.

Windows XP has many improvements incorporated into it which fall into several general categories. These are:

- Added features that make Windows XP load faster than any previous version of Windows, run more reliably, and the ability to return to a previous working version of the Operating System (similar to that under Windows Me).

- Improved Wizards (similar to those under Windows Me) let you set up home networks a lot easier and give you the ability to share Internet connections.

- Improved support for digital cameras, video recorders, and multimedia with an improved version of the Windows Media Player (now version 10).

- Improved features and tools in Internet Explorer 6 allow faster performance, and better Web communication from e-mail to instant messaging to video conferencing.

- Improved Windows File Protection which prevents the replacement of protected system files such as **.sys**, **.dll**, **.ocx**, **.ttf**, **.fon**, and **.exe** files, so that installing software does not corrupt the operating system by overwriting shared system files such as dynamic-link libraries (**.dll** files) and executable files (**.exe** files).

- Windows XP Professional also includes features for power users, such as enhanced file security, remote access to your computer's desktop and a personal Web server.

Since the release of Windows XP in 2001, there have been two major updates. The first one was Service Pack 1 (SP1) which contained updates for security issues, operating System reliability, application compatibility, and improved Windows XP Setup.

In August 2004, Microsoft released the second major update to Windows XP, Service Pack 2 (SP2). This update focuses mainly on the security of your computer, and is over 260 MB in size, so downloading it might take a rather long time, particularly if this is done via a 56k modem. Alternatively, you might be able to find a PC magazine that provides this update free on CD. We strongly recommend installing SP2.

Microsoft has made security the central theme of SP2, although there are some additional features that are not specifically geared to protecting your computer. The main visible changes are to be seen in the form of additional Control Panel utilities which allow you to:

- Automatically update windows XP by periodically checking its servers for new updates. This utility makes sure that you do not forget to update your Operating System and thus become compromised by virus attacks.

- Start a new, friendlier, Network Setup and Wireless Connection Wizards. Bluetooth support ensures easy communication with suitably equipped PDAs and mobile phones.

- Access a new Security Centre which monitors your PC's security settings with respect to its Firewall, Automatic Updates, and Virus protection. If your virus suite cannot be detected, then the Security Centre will let you know.

- Access and configure the new Windows firewall which is far more sophisticated than the old and rather weak Internet Connection Firewall.

- Outlook Express now includes the Attachment Execution Service which checks the safety of attachments in an effort to unify the approach to attachment security with that of Microsoft Outlook. Now, SP2 protects areas of memory where previously viruses could hide and execute without your knowledge.

Contents

1

Customising the Start Menu

At the top of the *start* menu the name of the current user is displayed with a picture against it. Left-clicking this picture opens the User Accounts screen shown in Fig. 1.1.

Fig. 1.1 The User Accounts Dialogue Box.

From here you can choose a different picture for the current user either from the ones supplied or from one of your own.

In Windows XP the first of its two-column *start* menu adapts to the way you use your PC - it keeps track of what features and programs you use the most and adds them to the list on the left column.

To remove an application from the first column of the *start* menu, right-click it and select **Remove from this List** as shown in Fig. 1.2 on the next page. This removes the name of the application from the list, not the application itself from your hard disc.

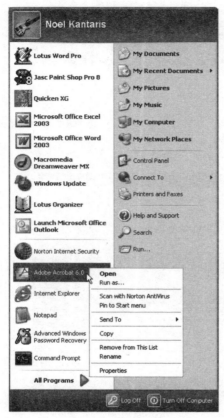

Fig. 1.2 The Start Menu.

As can be seen, you also have a menu option to **Pin to Start menu** any program. This adds it to the top of the left column of the *start* menu which is a more permanent list.

You can also use this facility to pin your favourite programs, even if these are to be found in the **All Programs** menu, thus customising the way you run your computer and cutting down the endless number of shortcuts that most users seem to place on the desktop.

Once you have pinned your chosen programs to the *start* menu, you could rename by right-clicking their entry on the list and selecting **Rename** from the drop-down menu. You could even change their order on the list. To move an item on the *start* menu, point to it to highlight it, then drag it with the right mouse button pressed to the desired position on the list.

2

Changing the Log on & Log off Settings

 To change the way you log on to your computer, double-click the **User Accounts** icon, shown here, in the **Control Panel**, to display the screen in Fig. 2.1.

Fig. 2.1 The User Accounts Dialogue Box.

Next, click the **Change the way users log on or off** to display the screen shown in Fig. 2.2 on the next page, and remove the check mark from the **Use the Welcome screen** box.

Now using the *start*, **Log Off** option and after the display of a confirmation box, Windows logs off the current user and displays the Log On to Windows dialogue box shown in Fig. 2.3 also on the next page. In the **User name** box change the name of the currently logged user to **Administrator**, type in the **Password**, and click **OK**.

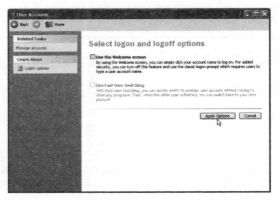

Fig. 2.2 Selecting the Log on and Log off Options.

Fig. 2.3 The Log On to Windows Box.

From now on, when you use the *start*, **Shut Down** option, you will be given several different options for shutting down Windows, as shown in Fig. 2.4. The currently logged user appears as the first option.

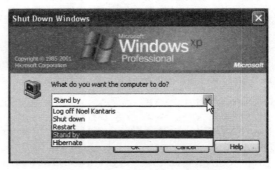

Fig. 2.4 The Shut Down Windows Dialogue Box.

3

Changing the Display Settings

If your display unit is capable of higher resolution than the 800 by 600 pixels (picture elements) required by Windows XP, you might like to increase its resolution to, say, 1024 by 768 pixels, or higher. This will allow you to see a larger number of icons on a screen when a given application is activated.

To change the display settings, use the *start*, **Control Panel** command, then in the **Classic** view, double-click the **Display** icon shown here. In the Display Properties dialogue box, click the Settings tab to display the screen in Fig. 3.1, in which the settings have been changed appropriately. For the new settings to take effect, click the **Apply** button followed by the **OK** button.

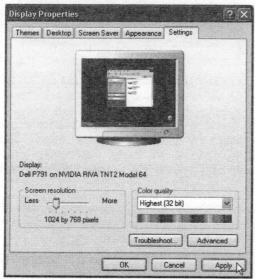

Fig. 3.1 The Settings Screen of the Display Properties Dialogue Box.

While the Display Properties dialogue box is open, you might like to explore the other available settings. For example:

Click the Themes tab to change the looks of your active windows. Selecting the Windows **Classic** view presents you with a display more akin to that of previous versions of Windows, as shown in Fig. 3.2 below.

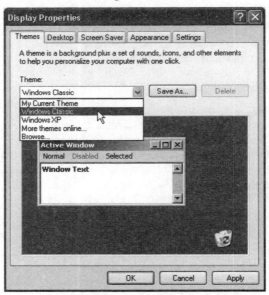

Fig. 3.2 The Themes Screen of the Display Properties Dialogue Box.

Click the Desktop tab to change the background of your desktop, which by default was set to 'Bliss'. The first four background options are quite interesting, or you could select your own - to fill the screen choose **Stretch** under **Position**.

Use the Screen Savers tab to select a different screen saver - you will be able to preview your selection before making a final choice.

Click the Appearance tab to select a different look for your windows and buttons, apply a different colour scheme and select a different font size.

4

Managing the Taskbar Icons

Activating the Quick Launch Icons

At the bottom of the Desktop screen is the Taskbar. It contains the *start* button which can be used to quickly start a program.

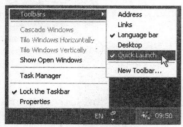

Fig. 4.1 Quick Launch Activation.

To activate the Quick Launch icons, right-click an empty part of the Taskbar, point to the **Toolbars** option which displays the sub-menu, shown in Fig. 4.1, and left-click the **Quick Launch** entry. This displays three icons next to the *start* button; left-clicking one of these, launches its application.

The default **Quick Launch** icons, in order of appearance, have the following functions:

Launch the Internet Explorer Browser.

Show Desktop.

Launch Windows Media Player.

Using Other Taskbar Buttons

When you open a program, or a window, a button for it is placed on the Taskbar, as shown in Fig. 4.2 below.

Fig. 4.2 The Windows Taskbar.

You can left-click your mouse on this button to make this the active program, or window, which displays in a darker shade of blue on the Taskbar. So, you can always see what windows you have open, which is the active one, and quickly switch between them. As more buttons are placed on the Taskbar their size shrinks slightly, but up to a point. After that common entries are grouped together with a number indicating the number of open windows.

To see details relating to a grouped button, left-click it to open a list of components, as shown in Fig. 4.3.

Another interesting Taskbar menu option is **Properties** (Fig. 4.1). This allows you to change the Taskbar and *start* menu options.

Fig. 4.3 Grouped Taskbar Entries.

The System Tray Icons

The Taskbar also shows the current time to the far right, the **Windows Messenger**, the **Options**, the **Restore** and the

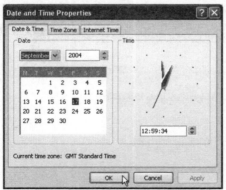

Language icons, as well as other icons added depending on your system. Moving the mouse pointer over the clock will display the date. Double-clicking the clock, opens the Date/Time Properties box, shown in Fig. 4.4, so that you can make changes, if necessary.

Fig. 4.4 Date and Time Properties Dialogue Box.

5

Recovering the Speaker Sound

Fig. 5.1 Left-click box.

If for some reason your PC's speakers go silent, then apart from checking that they are still connected correctly, you could left-click the **Volume** icon on your System tray (situated to the far right of the Task bar), pointed to in Fig. 5.1. On the displayed Volume dialogue box, make sure that the **Mute** box is not checked. If it is, click it to remove the check mark.

If the volume was not muted in Fig. 5.1, then double-click the **Volume** icon to display the expanded set of volume controls, as shown in Fig. 5.2 below.

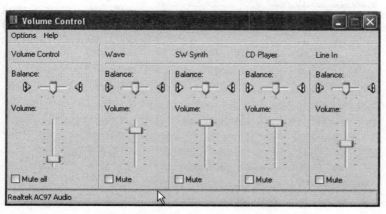

Fig. 5.2 The Expanded Volume Control Dialogue Box.

Check if any of the controls attached to the various devices are not muted, unless you meant to mute a specific device.

If this does not cure the problem, then right-click the **Volume** icon on your System tray to display the two-item menu shown in Fig. 5.3. Selecting the **Adjust Audio Properties** option, displays the screen in Fig. 5.4.

Fig. 5.3 Right-click box.

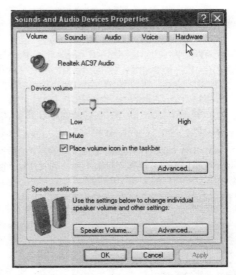

Fig. 5.4 The Expanded Volume Control Dialogue Box.

This multi-tab dialogue box gives you information specific to your system, which you might need if you seek external help. To check that everything is functioning correctly, click the Hardware tab, then select from the displayed list the appropriate audio device attached to your system and click the **Troubleshoot** button.

If after all this you still have silent speakers, it might be time to seek external help. At least you will be able to inform the person helping you exactly what you have done, and what type of audio devices are attached to your system.

6

Changing the Keyboard Language

Sometimes your system might be configured to a US keyboard, even though visually it appears to be a UK keyboard. You will know that this is the case when you type the £ key and the # symbol appears on your application screen.

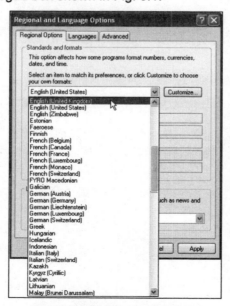

To change the language of your keyboard, use the **start**, **Control Panel** command and double-click the **Regional and Language Options** button, shown here, on the displayed screen. This opens the multi-tab dialogue box shown in Fig. 6.1.

Fig. 6.1 Selecting Regional Options.

On this dialogue box, select **English (United Kingdom)** and click the **Apply** button. Next, click the Languages tab and in the displayed screen, shown in Fig. 6.2, click the **Details** button to display Fig. 6.3.

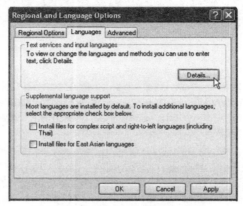

Fig. 6.2 The Languages Tab Screen.

Fig. 6.3 The Settings Tab Screen.

In Fig. 6.3, click the **Add** button to open the screen shown in Fig. 6.4, in which we have already selected **English (United Kingdom)** under the **Input language**.

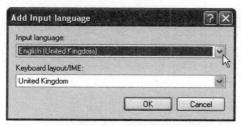

Fig. 6.4 Selecting the Input Language.

This allows you to select **English (United Kingdom - United Kingdom** in the Text Services and Input Languages dialogue box under the **Default input language**, as shown in Fig. 6.5 below.

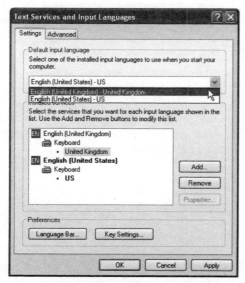

Fig. 6.5 Selecting the Default Input Language.

Finally, you can now highlight the unwanted language under the **Installed Services**, as shown in Fig. 6.6, and click the **Remove** button.

Fig. 6.6 Removing the Unwanted Language.

For these changes to take effect, click the **Apply** button, followed by **OK**. You might need to restart your computer to make these changes permanent.

7

Fixing the Caps Lock Key

How many times have you typed a sentence only to find that all letters in it are in capitals (apart from the first one, that is) because you accidentally touched the **Caps Lock** key - tHEN YOU HAVE TO TYPE IT ALL OVER AGAIN?

One way of dealing with this is to use the **Accessibility** option in the **Control Panel** and check the **Use ToggleKeys** box, pointed to in Fig. 7.1 below.

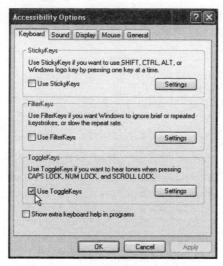

Fig. 7.1 The Accessibility Options Box.

Clicking the **Apply** button, activates the facility which emits a slight sound when you touch one of the three keys mentioned above. However, you must have good hearing, unless you turn up the speaker volume which you might find unacceptable when performing other operations.

Re-mapping the Caps Lock Key

You can re-map the **Caps Lock** key to perform the function of, say, the **Shift** key, thus disabling its normal function. However, this requires you to change values in the **Registry** by using some sort of program, of which there are several available, either free or for the payment of a very small amount.

To see for yourself what is available, log on to **google.com** and search for "Disable Caps Lock in Windows XP". A few of the 8,000 plus sites that are found are shown in Fig. 7.2.

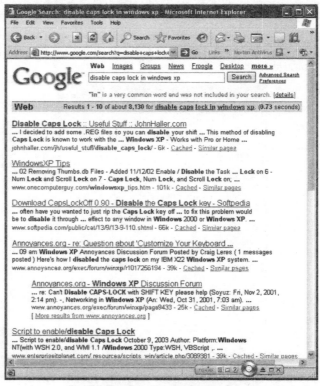

Fig. 7.2 The Results of a Google Search.

As you can see, the choice is endless, so we leave it to you to pick the one you trust.

8

Inserting Special Characters in Documents

The Windows Character Map

A useful feature in Windows is the Character Map, shown open in Fig. 8.1 below. This should be found by clicking *start*, then selecting **All Programs, Accessories, System Tools, Character Map** from the Windows cascade menu.

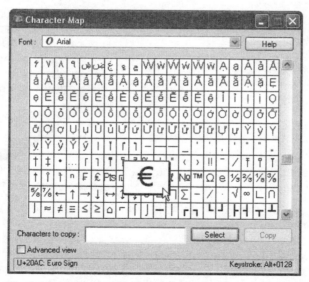

Fig. 8.1 Selecting a Character from the Character Map Utility.

You use this facility from an application, such as a word processor, when you need a special character, such as the 'Euro' sign € above, to be included in your document.

To copy a special character, not found on your keyboard, into your document, open the Character Map, select the **Font**, as shown in Fig. 8.2, and click the character to enlarge it, as shown in Fig. 8.1.

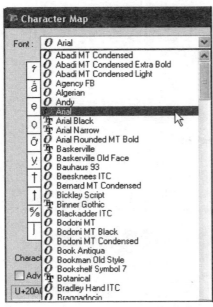

Fig. 8.2 Selecting a Font in Character Map.

Next, click the **Select** button, which places the selected character in the **Characters to copy** box, and when you have all the characters you want in this box, click the **Copy** button to copy them to the clipboard. Now, return to your application, make sure the insertion point is in the correct position and paste the characters there.

Character Map Shortcuts

The method described above of inserting special characters in your document works well, but there are some shortcuts that are extremely useful, particularly with respect to the Euro sign.

To insert the Euro sign in your document, just use the **Alt Gr+4** key combination where the **Alr Gr** key is found to the right of the space bar, and the number **4** is the keyboard 4, not the keypad 4. The advantage of this method (apart from being less cumbersome), is that the font size is automatically adjusted to the font size of the the rest of your document - just like this; €.

Also note that using the **Alt Gr** key with any vowel will put an acute accent on the vowel, such as the é in hélas. For all other types of accents on letters you must use the Character Map.

9

Adding New Software

To add new Windows programs to your computer's hard disc, use the ***start***, **Control Panel** command, and click the **Add or Remove Programs** icon, shown here. This examines your hard disc for installed programs and displays its contents in a window similar to the one shown in Fig. 9.1 below.

Add or
Remove
Programs

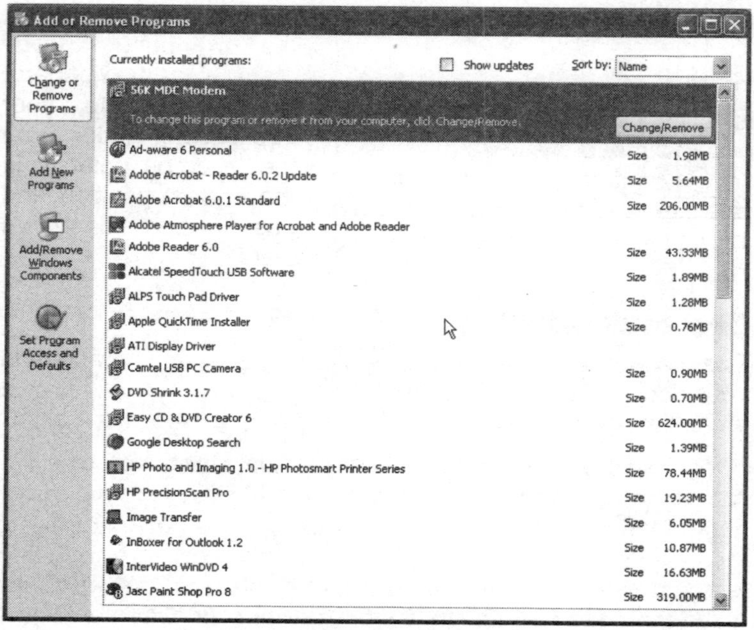
Add or Remove Programs
Change or Remove Programs
Add New Programs
Add/Remove Windows Components
Set Program Access and Defaults
Currently installed programs:
Show updates
Sort by: Name
56K MDC Modem
To change this program or remove it from your computer, click Change/Remove.
Change/Remove
Ad-aware 6 Personal Size 1.98MB
Adobe Acrobat - Reader 6.0.2 Update Size 5.64MB
Adobe Acrobat 6.0.1 Standard Size 206.00MB
Adobe Atmosphere Player for Acrobat and Adobe Reader
Adobe Reader 6.0 Size 43.33MB
Alcatel SpeedTouch USB Software Size 1.89MB
ALPS Touch Pad Driver Size 1.28MB
Apple QuickTime Installer Size 0.76MB
ATI Display Driver
Camtel USB PC Camera Size 0.90MB
DVD Shrink 3.1.7 Size 0.70MB
Easy CD & DVD Creator 6 Size 624.00MB
Google Desktop Search Size 1.39MB
HP Photo and Imaging 1.0 - HP Photosmart Printer Series Size 78.44MB
HP PrecisionScan Pro Size 19.23MB
Image Transfer Size 6.05MB
InBoxer for Outlook 1.2 Size 10.87MB
InterVideo WinDVD 4 Size 16.63MB
Jasc Paint Shop Pro 8 Size 319.00MB

Fig. 9.1 The Add or Remove Programs Screen.

In your case, this list of programs will most certainly be different.

Next, click the **Add New Programs** button on the left pane of the displayed dialogue box, which changes to the one shown in Fig. 9.2.

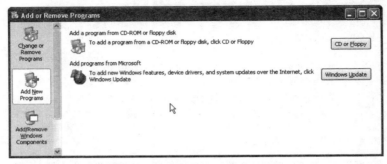

Fig. 9.2 The Add New Programs Screen.

This facility to add programs seems superfluous because installing new Windows programs on your computer's hard disc is made very easy these days. Almost all Windows applications are distributed on one or more CDs the first one of which uses an auto-run program which in turn runs the Setup program.

Furthermore, most applications vendors give you instructions that if the auto-run program does not start the installation process, to click the Windows *start* button, and select the **Run** command which opens the Run dialogue box shown in Fig. 9.3, and type in the **Open** text box the command

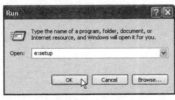

Fig. 9.3 The Run Dialogue Box.

```
e:\setup
```

where e: is our CD-ROM drive; yours will probably be different. Clicking the **OK** button, starts the installation process.

In the end, which method you use, if the auto-run facility fails, is up to you.

10

Adding or Removing Windows Features

To add or remove Windows features, use the *start*, **Control Panel** command, and click the **Add or Remove Programs** icon, shown here to the left. This examines your hard disc for installed programs and displays its contents in a window similar to the one shown in Fig. 10.1 below.

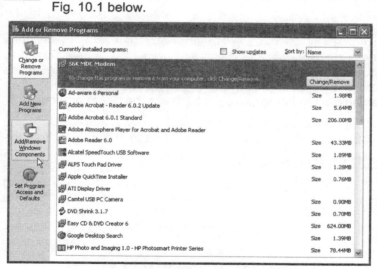

Fig. 10.1 The Add or Remove Programs Screen.

The **Add/Remove Windows Components** icon, pointed to in Fig. 10.1, allows you to install or remove specific Windows components at any time. Clicking this icon, opens the dialogue box shown in Fig. 10.2 on the next page. Next, highlight the group that you think will contain what you want to add or remove, and click the **Details** button.

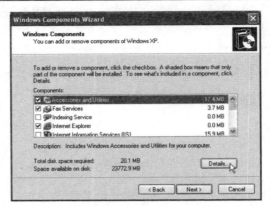

Fig. 10.2 The Windows Components Wizard.

This examines your system and lists the components of the chosen group, as shown in Fig. 10.3. Clicking the box to the left of an item name will install the selected component, while any items with their ticks removed, will be uninstalled.

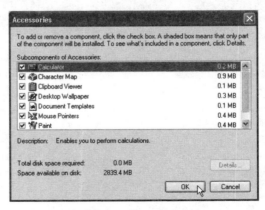

Fig. 10.3 The Accessories Dialogue Box.

You will need to have the original Windows XP CD available, and when you have made the selections you want, keep clicking **OK** to carry out the required changes. It is easy to use up too much hard disc space with Windows XP features, so keep your eye on the **Total disk space required** entry.

11

Saving Power

You can automatically put your computer into hibernation or standby, provided you log on as an administrator, and your computer is set up by the manufacturer to support these options. If your computer is connected to a network, remember that network policy settings may prevent you from completing these tasks.

Hibernation Mode

When your computer is put into hibernation mode, everything in the computer memory is saved on your hard disc, and your computer is switched off. When you turn the computer back on, all programs and documents that were open when you turned the computer off are restored on the desktop.

To initiate hibernation, activate the **Control Panel** and double-click the **Power Options** icon shown here. Then, in the displayed Power Options Properties dialogue box, click the Hibernate tab. If the Hibernate tab is unavailable, then this is because your computer does not support this feature. If it does, make sure the **Enable hibernation** box is checked, as shown in Fig. 11.1 on the next page.

Next, click the Advanced tab and select what you want under **Options**, then click the down-arrow button against the **When I press the power button on my computer** box and choose what you want to happen from the drop-down options list in Fig. 11.2 also shown on the next page.

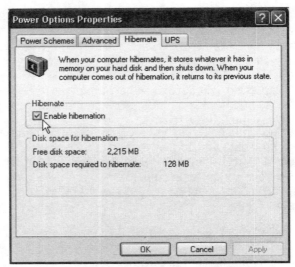

Fig. 11.1 The Power Options Properties Screen.

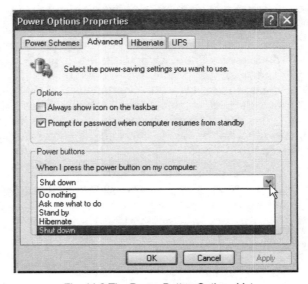

Fig. 11.2 The Power Button Options List.

Finally, click the Power Schemes tab, and select a time in **System hibernates**, as shown in Fig. 11.3. If you set this to, say, 'after 1 min', then you can sit back and see what happens. With our system, after one minute we were informed that it was safe to switch off the computer, which we did. When switching on the computer a few seconds later, Windows XP started up automatically and loaded all the programs that happened to be loaded at the time of hibernation.

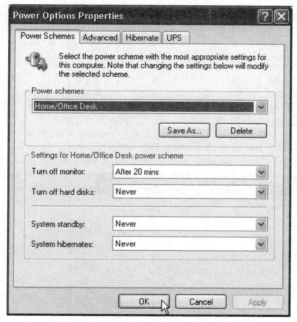

Fig. 11.3 The Power Options Power Schemes Screen.

Obviously this is a time saver much favoured by users of laptop computers. However, there is no reason why users of desktop computers should not also be in favour of this power saving management.

If you decide that you do not want your system to hibernate, just go through the procedure described above and uncheck the selected option in the Power Options Properties screen of Fig. 11.1. Finally, click the Power Schemes tab, and select 'never' for the time the **System hibernates**.

Standby Mode

When your computer is put into standby mode, information in computer memory is not saved to your hard disc. You must save all your work before putting your computer into standby mode, because if there is an interruption in power, all information in the computer's memory will be lost.

To initiate standby mode, activate the Control Panel and click on the Power Options icon. In the displayed Power Options Properties dialogue box, click the Power Schemes tab, as shown in Fig. 11.3.

If you are using a portable computer, you can specify one setting for battery power and a different setting for AC power. In fact, you can adjust any power management option that your computer's hardware configuration supports.

12

Configuring a Printer

To configure your printer, left-click the **Printers and Faxes** icon in the *start* cascade menu, select the printer you want to configure, and click the **Set printer properties** option in the **Printer Tasks** list pointed to in Fig. 12.1 below. This opens the Properties dialogue box for the selected printer.

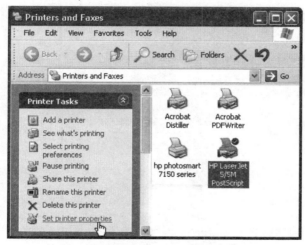

Fig. 12.1 The Printer and Faxes Window.

From the displayed tabbed dialogue box you can control all the printer's parameters, such as the printer port (or network path), paper and graphics options, built-in fonts, and other device options specific to the printer model. All these settings are fairly self explanatory and as they depend on your printer type, we will leave them to you.

A newly installed printer is automatically set as the default printer, indicated by a tick against it. To change this, select a printer connected to your PC, right-click it, and choose the **Set as Default Printer** option on the displayed shortcut menu.

Once you have installed and configured your printers in Windows they are then available for all your application programs to use. The correct printer is selected usually in one of the application's **File** menu options.

Managing Print Jobs

If you want to find out what exactly is happening while a document or documents are being sent to your printer, double-click the printer icon on the right end of the Task bar, to open its window.

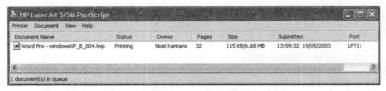

Fig. 12.2 The Print Queue Window.

As shown in Fig. 12.2, this displays detailed information about the contents of any work actually being printed, or of print jobs that are waiting in the queue. This includes the name of the document, its status and 'owner', when it was added to the print queue, the printing progress and when printing was started.

You can control the printing operation from the **Printer** and **Document** menu options of the Print Queue window, from the object menu, or from the **Printer Tasks** list. Selecting **Printer, Pause Printing** will stop the operation until you make the same selection again; it is a toggle menu option. The **Cancel All Documents** option will remove all, or selected, print jobs from the print queue. However, be patient as the deleting process takes its time.

13

Installing a Fax Printer

Windows XP includes its own Fax printer driver. To install it click the **Install a local fax printer** option in the Printer Tasks box as shown in Fig. 13.1 below.

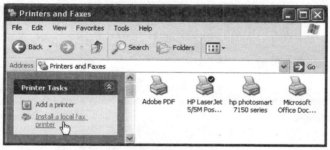

Fig. 13.1 The Printers and Faxes Dialogue box.

This starts the **Install Fax Wizard** which might ask for the Windows XP distribution CD so that required files can be copied. Once that is done and you supply the information you want to be included in your faxes, a Fax printer is installed in the **Printers and Faxes** folder, as shown in Fig. 13.2 below.

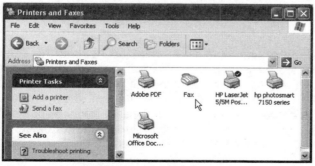

Fig. 13.2 The New Fax Icon.

The Fax Utility

To fax a text document or graphic image, use the Fax utility, which supports scanned graphic images and will automatically convert graphics to the appropriate file format before you send them. To send and receive faxes, you need a fax device, such as a fax modem - it must support fax capabilities, not just data standards. Once the Fax Printer is installed, you can send faxes from a local fax device attached to your computer, or with a remote fax device connected to fax resources located on a network.

If you have a fax device installed, click *start*, then select **All Programs, Accessories, Communications, Fax** to display the available command options shown in Fig. 13.3.

Fig. 13.3 The Fax Menu Options.

Use the **Fax Console** option to display incoming and outgoing faxes and view and manage your faxes. Clicking this option displays the screen shown in Fig. 13.4.

Fig. 13.4 The Fax Console Screen.

Use the **File** menu options to send a fax (it starts the **Send Fax Wizard** asking you for the recipient's name and other details - you can use the information held in your Address Book, and specify multiple recipients for the one fax), receive a fax now, view, print, save and mail a fax. While a fax is being sent, you can pause or resume its transmission, restart or delete it. You can also import sent or received faxes into the Fax Console.

14

Creating a New Folder

To create a new folder within, say **My Documents**, use the *start*, **My Documents** menu option to display Fig. 14.1 below (in your case the contents of this folder will most likely be different). Then

- Point to the **Make a new folder** entry on the **Tasks** pane and when it changes to a hand, as shown in Fig. 14.1 below, left-click it.

Fig. 14.1 Creating a New Folder.

Naming a New Folder

* When Windows creates a new folder it places it at the end of the list of existing folders and names it **New Folder**, highlighting its name and waiting for you to name it, as shown here.

* Type a name, say, Photos, which replaces the default name given to it by Windows. If this doesn't happen, don't worry, you must have clicked the left mouse button an extra time which fixes the default name (see below how to rename it)

Renaming a Folder or a File

Method 1

* Left-click the folder or file you want to rename to select it.

* Left-clicking it once more will display the insertion pointer within its name. Type a different name to replace the existing one.

Method 2

* Left-click the folder or file you want to rename to select it (in this example we chose a folder).

* Left-click the **Rename this folder** entry on the **Tasks** menu, shown in Fig. 14.2, which causes the insertion pointer to be displayed within its name. Type a different name to replace the existing one.

Fig. 14.2 Renaming a Folder.

15

Expanding All Items in a Folder

When you use **My Computer** to look at a folder, say **My Documents**, the displayed screen might look something similar, but not identical, to the one in Fig. 15.1.

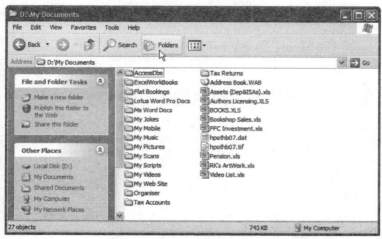

Fig. 15.1 The Contents of My Documents Folder.

If you now click the **Folders** icon on the Tools bar, pointed to in the screen above, the display changes to the one shown in Fig. 15.2 on the next page. The + sign in front of the **My Documents** folder, pointed to in Fig. 15.2, indicates that there are sub-folders associated with these folders which can be seen by clicking the + sign. In our case, doing so reveals sub-folders which will then have their + sign clicked to open each in turn.

To automatically open all the sub-folders below a chosen folder, press the '*' key on the numeric pad of the keyboard. The result is shown in Fig. 15.3 on the next page.

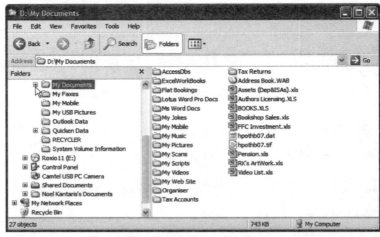

Fig. 15.2 The Folders View of My Documents.

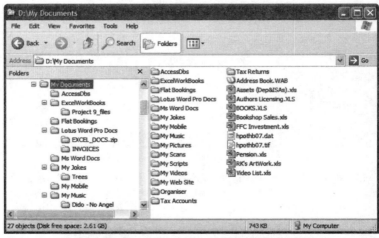

Fig. 15.3 The Open Sub-folders Under a Selected Folder.

Pressing the '-' key and the '+' key on the numeric pad of the keyboard, closes and opens, respectively, one level of sub-folders under the selected folder. This method also works with the **Registry**, after running **regedit**.

16

Searching for Files & Folders

In order to demonstrate how to search for files (or folders) we need to already have some files, common to both us and you, that we can work with. To do this, we will search our hard disc for picture files hopefully provided to all Windows XP users.

To search for files, click *start* and select the **Search** menu option. This opens the Search Dialogue box, the left panel of which is shown in Fig. 16.1. Next, click the **All files and folders** entry in the Tasks pane (as shown in Fig. 16.1).

Fig. 16.1 Specifying Type of Search.

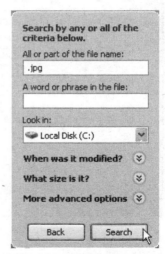

Fig. 16.2 Specifying the Item and Drive for a Search.

You now need to specify the name (or part of it - see next page) of the item you are searching for and the drive you want to search (in this case the drive where Windows is installed on your PC), as shown in Fig. 16.2.

In our search criteria we specified, in Fig. 16.2, that part of the filename we want to search for is **.jpg** which indicates we are interested in graphic files. Other popular filename extensions are:

.bak	a backup file
.exe	an executable file
.hlp	a hypertext help file
.html	a hypertext markup language file
.jpeg or **.jpg**	a graphic format file
.rtf	a rich text format file
.sys	a system file
.tmp or **.temp**	a temporary file
.txt	a basic text file
.wav	a waveform of a soundbite.

Left-clicking the **Search** button, produces the list of files shown in Fig. 16.3 below.

Fig. 16.3 Search Results for .jpg Files.

What is displayed above is a fraction of the total files found by this particular search. You might have to scroll down a bit to find what appears above, which are part of the contents of the **Windows\Web\Wallpaper** folder.

17

Downloading Pictures from a Camera

Almost all digital cameras come with software that helps you download pictures to your PC. However, you can do the same thing with Windows XP without having to install any additional software. To achieve this, do the following:

* Connect your camera to your computer (usually via a USB cable) and turn it on, which displays the screen in Fig. 17.1.

Fig. 17.1 The Windows Auto Detect Utility.

The PC has detected the Camera's Memory Stick, the contents of which can be displayed by clicking the **OK** button, as shown on the left panel in Fig. 17.2 on the next page.

17 Downloading Pictures from a Camera

(a) (b)

Fig. 17.2 (a) The Memory Stick Contents and (b) A Test Folder on the PC.

On the right panel of Fig. 17.2 we show a Test Folder we created on our PC's hard disc in which we dragged one of the picture files from the camera's Memory Stick.

To copy all the files in the camera's Memory Stick, highlight them all and drag them to the chosen folder on your computer.

18

Viewing Pictures & Other Images

In Fig. 18.1 below, the contents of the **My Pictures** folder are shown as **Thumbnails** with both the **View** sub-menu, and the right-click menu of a selected image also shown open.

Fig. 18.1 The My Pictures Folder Displayed in Thumbnail View.

Images can be arranged by name, size, type, etc., from the **View** menu, or can be previewed, rotated, set as desktop background, or opened in a variety of imaging programs, from its shortcut menu. This can be very useful, particularly if you have installed a graphics program that assumes you will be using it to open all available image file types.

File Association

When you install a graphics program it might associate itself with all the file types it uses, irrespective of any current file associations. To change this, right-click on a given type of file, say a **.jpg** file, and select the **Properties** option to open the dialogue box shown in Fig. 18.2.

In the General tab sheet of the Properties box, click the **Change** button to open the dialogue box shown in Fig. 18.3. From here you can select the program you would like to open this type of file.

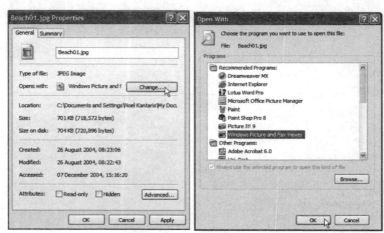

Fig. 18.2 The Properties Dialogue Box.   Fig. 18.3 The Open With Dialogue Box.

If you want the selected program to always open this type of file, make sure the box to the left of the **Browse** button is checked.

Previewing an Image in the Picture & Fax Viewer

If you double-click an image or select **Preview** from its right-click menu, then that image is displayed enlarged in the Windows **Picture and Fax Viewer** (provided it was associated with this type of file), as shown in Fig. 18.4.

Fig. 18.4 The Windows Picture and Fax Viewer.

The buttons at the bottom of the screen of the Windows **Picture and Fax Viewer** can be used to navigate through your pictures folder, select the viewing size, view the pictures in your folder as a slide show, zoom in or out, rotate the image, and generally carry out certain housekeeping functions, including the opening of the picture in Microsoft Paint, so that you can edit it.

The Windows **Picture and Fax Viewer** can of course be used with other image documents including scanned pictures, digital camera photos or fax documents.

The Filmstrip View

To see your photos in another interesting display, use the **View**, **Filmstrip** command. To get the full benefit of this view, you need to increase the size of the displayed window to at least ¾ of the size of your screen, as shown in Fig. 18.5.

As each image is selected, an enlarged view of it displays above the filmstrip. The four buttons below the enlarged view can be used to navigate to the previous or the next image, and to rotate the selected image clockwise or anticlockwise.

Fig. 18.5 Photos Displayed in Filmstrip View.

You can also use the **Picture Task** menu to view images as a slide show, set a selected image as a desktop background, print a selected image, or copy selected images to a CD.

19

Copying Files & Folders to CD

What is demonstrated below with files, using the contents of **My Pictures** folder, could also be done with folders, or a mixture of files and folders within any folder.

Selecting Files and Folders

To select several objects, or icons, you have three options:

(a) If they form a contiguous list, left-click the first in the list, then with the **Shift** key depressed, click the last in the list.

(b) To select random objects hold the **Ctrl** key down and left-click them, one by one, as shown in Fig. 19.1 below.

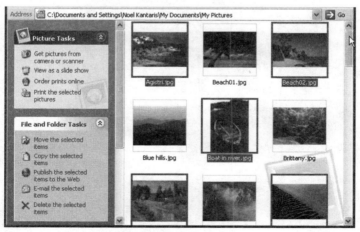

Fig. 19.1 Selecting Items in a Folder.

(c) To select all the items in a window use the **Edit**, **Select All** menu command, or the **Ctrl+A** keystrokes.

To cancel a selection, click in an empty area of the window.

Copying Selected Objects to CD

To copy (burn) files or folders to a CD, you will need a recordable compact disc (CD-R) or a rewritable compact disc (CD-RW) and a CD recorder.

To start the process, insert a blank recordable or rewritable CD in the CD recorder, then use the **View**, **Details** menu option to make sure that the selected files or folder contents do not exceed the CD's capacity (650 MB for a standard CD).

Next, click the **Copy the selected items** link, pointed to under **File and Folder Tasks**, as shown in Fig. 19.2, which displays the size of the files.

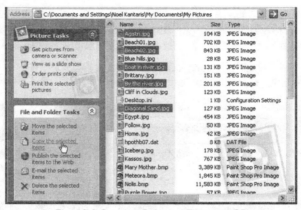

Fig. 19.2 Copying Selected Files to a CD.

Fig. 19.3 The Copy Items Box.

On the displayed Copy Items dialogue box, click the **CD Drive** link, followed by the **Copy** button, to start the copying process - you will be notified when it is completed. This method is excellent for making backups of your important data.

20

Compressing Files & Folders

Compressing files and folders allows you to greatly increase

Fig. 20.1 Creating a Zipped Folder.

the storage capacity of your hard disc and increases the amount of data you can copy on a single CD.

To start the process, open the drive or folder in which you want to create a compressed folder, say within **My Documents**, then use the **File, New** menu command, and select the **Compressed (zipped) Folder** option from the drop-down menu, as shown in Fig. 20.1.

The created folder has the extension **.zip** and you must retain this when renaming it. We renamed our folder **My Scans.zip** because, as an example, we will use data held on one of our computers, in a folder called **My Scans** which is just over 50 MB in size, and send it to the compressed folder we created. Of course, you could use your own folder for this example.

Next, open **My Computer** and locate the original **My Scans** (or your own) folder. In our case the folder is to be found in **My Documents**. We then used the **Edit, Select All** menu command and dragged the highlighted files into the newly renamed folder, as shown in Fig. 20.2 on the next page.

Fig. 20.2 Dragging a File into a Compressed Folder.

Releasing the mouse button displays the Compressing dialogue box and starts the process. Other files and folders can be sent to the compressed folder by dragging them onto it. Selected files are then compressed one at time before they are moved into the folder, while the contents of the dragged folders are also compressed.

To find out the size of the folder's contents before and after compression, double-click the compressed folder, use the **Edit**, **Select All** menu command, right-click on the highlighted files and select **Properties** from the drop-down menu. In our example, the size of the original 34 files is displayed as 52.164 MB, while its packed size as 40.546 MB. Some types of files compress even more.

You can open files and programs in a compressed folder by double-clicking them. If a program requires **.dll** (dynamic link library) or data files to run, then those files must first be extracted. To extract a file or folder from a compressed folder, simply drag it to its new location. To extract all files and folders within a compressed folder, right-click the folder and select **Extract All**. In the Extract Wizard you can specify where you want these files and folders to be extracted to.

When you compress files or folders as explained earlier, the original files or folders remain on your hard disc. To remove such files and folders from the originating disc or folder you must delete them.

21

Compressing & Sending Pictures via E-mail

Digital camera (or scanned) pictures can be extremely large in size (over 2 MB each). Sending a few of these without compressing them to a friend, might sorely test your friendship!

To reduce the size of each picture automatically, use **My Computer** to locate them, select the ones you want to include as attachments to an e-mail, right-click them and choose the **Send To** option on the drop-down menu, followed by the **Mail Recipient option**, as shown in Fig. 21.1.

Fig. 21.1 Sending Selected Pictures to a Mail Recipient.

This opens the Send Pictures via E-Mail dialogue box in which you can choose the **Make all my pictures smaller** option, as shown in Fig. 21.2. The **Show more options** link lets you set the picture size to send, from **Small** to **Large**.

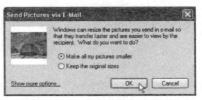

Fig. 21.2 The Send Pictures via E-mail Box.

Clicking the **OK** button starts the shrinking process (provided your e-mail program is not loaded), and after a few seconds the new e-mail message screen, shown in Fig. 21.3, is displayed ready with your re-sized attachments.

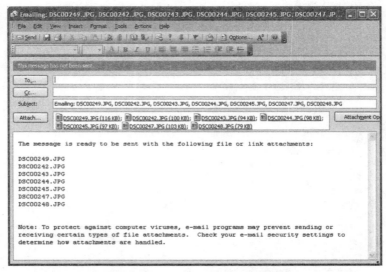

Fig. 21.3 The New E-mail Message with Attachments.

Note that the attached pictures have been reduced in size from a total of 15.5 MB to about 700 KB. Clicking the **Send** button sends the e-mail to the **Outbox** folder of your e-mail program.

22

Adding Items to the SendTo Folder

As we have seen in the previous chapter, a very useful feature of Windows is the ability to quickly send selected files and folders to specific destinations by right-clicking such a selection and choosing the **Send To** option on the drop-down menu, which opens the list of available destinations, as shown in Fig. 22.1

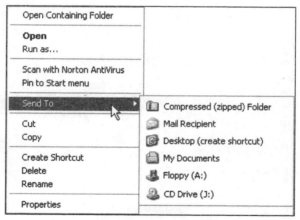

Fig. 22.1 Sending Folders and Files.

It is easy to add more locations to the **Send To** menu, as it is controlled by the contents of the **SendTo** folder, which is itself in the **Windows** folder. However, the **SendTo** folder is hidden by default, so if you use the *start*, **Search** command, you may not find it. To make it visible, start **My Computer**, then use the **Tools, Folder Options** command, click the View tab and finally click the **Show hidden files and folders** option.

To add a destination to the **Send To** menu use **My Computer** to do the following:

- Click the **Documents and Settings** folder on the drive where Windows XP is installed.

- Double-click the folder of a specific user.

- Double-click the **SendTo** folder.

- Use the **File, New, Shortcut** command as shown in Fig. 22.2 below.

Fig. 22.2 Adding a Shortcut to the SendTo Folder.

- Finally, follow the instructions on your screen.

23

Moving Files & Settings

To move your data files and personal settings from your old PC to the new one, without having to go through the same configuration you did with your old PC, then you need to use the Files and Settings Transfer Wizard. The Wizard can quickly move your personal display properties, **Taskbar and Folder** options, and Internet browser and mail settings. Other folders and files that are also moved are **My Documents**, **My Pictures**, and **Favorites**. The transfer can be carried out either by a direct cable connection between the two computers, via a floppy drive or other removable media, or a network drive.

To start the process, run the Files and Settings Transfer Wizard on both your old and new PC. To do this on your old machine, place the Windows XP distribution CD in its CD-ROM drive and on the first installation screen click the **Perform additional tasks** option to open the screen in Fig. 23.1.

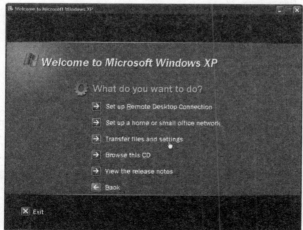

Fig. 23.1 Selecting the Transfer Files and Setting Option.

On that screen, click the **Transfer files and settings** option to start the Wizard on your old machine.

To open the Files and Settings Transfer Wizard on your new machine, use the *start*, **All Programs, Accessories, System Tools** command, then click the **Files and Settings Transfer Wizard** option. This opens the first screen of the Wizard, as shown in Fig. 23.2.

Fig. 23.2 The Files and Settings Transfer Wizard.

In subsequent Wizard screens, on both machines, you are told:

· To state whether this is your new or old computer.

To state which media you want to use for the creation of a Wizard disc which will contain all your relevant files and settings.

To specify which files and folders you want to transfer. Don't go overboard with your selection here as it could take a very long time to accomplish the task.

To go to the new computer with the newly created disc start the Wizard and complete the transfer.

24

Keeping a Hard Disc Healthy

Cleaning up a Fixed Hard Disc

To start the **Disk Cleanup** utility, use the *start*, **All Programs**,

 Accessories, **System Tools** menu, and click its icon, shown here, on the cascade menu. The utility then asks you to select the fixed drive you want to clean up,

 as in Fig. 24.1. It then scans the specified drive, and then lists temporary files, Internet cache files, and unnecessary program files that you can safely delete, as shown in Fig. 24.2 below.

Fig. 24.1 Selecting a Drive.

Fig. 24.2 Files Found by Cleanup.

In our case, we could free 47,253 KB of disc space by simply deleting the Temporary Internet Files (Web pages stored on the hard disc for quick viewing). The More Options tab allows you to remove Windows components and installed programs that you do not use any more.

Scanning a Fixed Hard Disc for Errors

To check, and if possible repair, the integrity of a fixed hard disc, click **My Computer** then in the displayed screen right-click the fixed drive you want to check, select **Properties** from the drop-down menu and click the Tools tab to display the screen in Fig. 24.3.

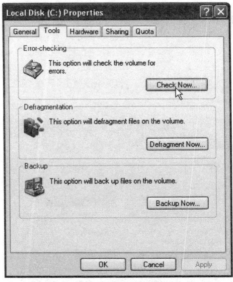

Fig. 24.3 The Disk Properties Screen.

You have three choices; **Check Now** for disc errors, **Defragment Now**, or **Backup Now**. The last option is not available by default in the Windows XP Home edition.

Before you start scanning your selected drive for errors, or start defragmenting it, close all running programs and applications on that drive.

25

Using the Backup Utility

Windows XP comes with a Backup Utility which is installed by default in the Professional Edition, but has to be installed manually in the Home Edition. The Backup utility is included on the Windows XP Home Edition CD-ROM in the ValueAdd folder, but it does not support the **Automated System Recovery Wizard**.

To manually install Backup:

* Double-click the NTBackup.msi file in the

  e:\ValueAdd\msft\NTBackup

  location on the Windows XP Home Edition CD, where e: is our CD-ROM drive (yours might be different).

* Follow the instructions of the Wizard and when installation is complete, click **Finish**.

The Backup utility is accessible via the *start*, **All Programs**, **Accessories**, **System Tools** cascade menu. It is a utility that can be used to back up both system set-up and data files from the hard disc to another, removable storage medium, on a regular basis.

Hard discs can 'crash' (but not as often now as they used to) and your computer could be stolen, or lost in a fire or flood. Any of these events would cause a serious data loss, particularly to businesses, unless you had backed it all up, and stored it somewhere safely, preferably away from the vicinity of your computer.

Making a Backup

To make a backup of your data, use the *start*, **All Programs**, **Accessories**, **System Tools**, cascade menu command and click the **Backup** icon, shown here, which starts the **Backup or Restore Wizard**, as shown in Fig. 25.1.

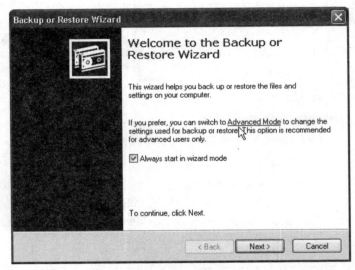

Fig. 25.1 The Windows XP Professional Backup Welcome Screen.

Note the **Advanced Mode** link pointed to in Fig. 25.1 above. Clicking on this link allows you to schedule backups. We will look at this facility in the next chapter.

The backup procedure can be carried out on a tape, a floppy disc, or a removable disc. Click the **Next** button to display the second Wizard screen where you can choose to **Back up files and settings**, while in the third Wizard screen you can select what to back up. In the fourth Wizard screen, you can then select the folders you want to back up by clicking the + sign to open its structure in the left-hand pane, then double-clicking any sub-folder to check it.

Restoring a Backup

To restore folders or files that have been previously backed up, place the first disc of the set in the disc drive, activate the **Backup or Restore Wizard** and on the second Wizard screen click the Restore radio button followed by **Next**. Again, click the + sign to open the file structure in the left-hand pane of the Restore window, as shown in Fig. 25.2. In this way you can choose to restore individual components of the backup set.

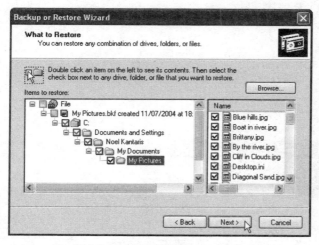

Fig. 25.2 Selecting the Backup Set to Restore.

Pressing the **Next** button, displays a Summary screen of the restore procedure. Clicking the **Advanced** button on this Summary screen, gives you a choice on where to restore the selected items, then what to do when restoring files that already exist, as shown in Fig. 25.3 on the next page.

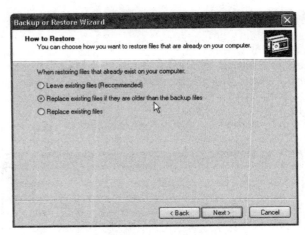

Fig. 25.3 Selecting How to Restore.

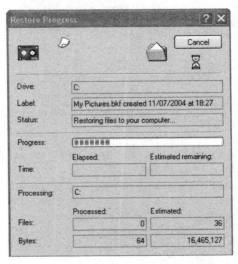

Fig. 25.4 The Restore Progress Screen.

A good choice would be to select the option to 'Replace the file on disk only if it is older than the backup copy'. After making an appropriate selection on file replacement and file security, pressing the **Finish** button causes the Wizard to start the restore process, as shown in Fig. 25.4.

26

Choosing a Backup Type

To see what types of backup exist, first activate the Backup or Restore Wizard by using the *start*, **All Programs**, **Accessories**, **System Tools**, cascade menu command and clicking the **Backup** icon, shown here. In the displayed **Backup or Restore Wizard** screen, shown in Fig. 26.1, click the **Advanced Mode** link pointed to in the figure.

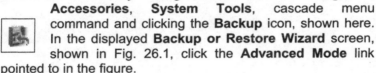

Fig. 26.1 The Windows XP Professional Backup Welcome Screen.

Clicking on this link allows you to schedule backups and see what types of backup exist on the displayed screen in Fig. 26.2, shown on the next page.

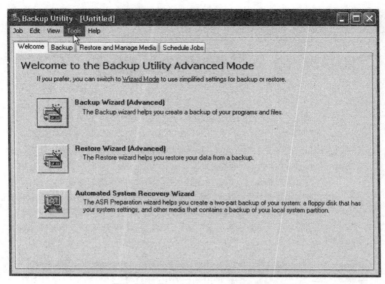

Fig. 26.2 The Advanced Backup Utility.

Next, use the **Tools, Options** command to open the Options dialogue box shown in Fig. 26.3 below.

Fig. 26.3 Selecting the Backup Type.

The Backup utility supports five methods of backing up data on your computer or network. These are:

Normal Backup
Copies all selected files and marks them as having been backed up. With normal backups, you need only the most recent copy of the backup file or tape to restore all of the files. A normal backup is usually performed the first time you create a backup set.

Copy Backup
Copies all selected files but does not mark them as having been backed up. Copying is useful if you want to back up files between normal and incremental backups because it does not affect these other backup operations.

Differential Backup
Copies files created or changed since the last normal or incremental backup. It does not mark files as having been backed up. If you are performing a combination of normal and differential backups, restoring files and folders requires that you have the last normal as well as the last differential backup.

Incremental Backup
Backs up only those files created or changed since the last normal or incremental backup. It marks files as having been backed up. If you use a combination of normal and incremental backups, you will need to have the last normal backup set as well as all incremental backup sets in order to restore your data.

Daily Backup
Copies all selected files that have been modified the day the daily backup is performed. The backed-up files are not marked as having been backed up.

If the data files you are backing up are not very large in size, then using a normal backup is the easiest method. The backup set is stored on one disc or tape and restoring data from it is very easy.

If the amount of your storage space is limited, then back up your data using a combination of normal and incremental backups; it is the quickest method. However, recovering files can be time-consuming and difficult because the backup set can be stored on several discs or tapes.

Finally, backing up your data using a combination of normal and differential backups is more time-consuming, especially if your data changes frequently, but it is easier to restore the data because the backup set is usually stored on only a few discs or tapes.

27

Scheduling Tasks

Using the *start*, **All Programs**, **Accessories**, **System Tools**,
cascade menu command and clicking the **Schedule
Tasks** icon, displays the screen in Fig. 27.1 below.

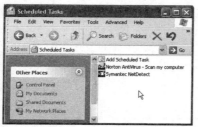

From here you carry out
several house-keeping
tasks, such as data
backup, or disc cleanup,
at times convenient to
you.

If you are running other
programs, such as Norton
AntiVirus in our case, an
entry for that program also

Fig. 27.1 The Scheduled Tasks Window.

appears in the Scheduled window (Fig. 27.1).

To add a scheduled task, double-click the **Add Scheduled
Task** icon to start the Wizard. Clicking **Next** on the first Wizard
screen displays the second Wizard screen, shown in Fig. 27.2.

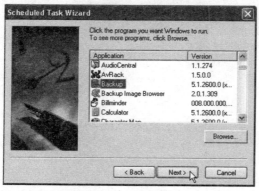

Fig. 27.2 The Second Scheduled Task Wizard Screen.

On the screen in Fig. 27.2, select the task to be scheduled then click the **Next** button to display the third Wizard screen, as shown in Fig. 27.3, in which you are asked to specify the frequency at which you would like the selected task to be performed (we selected weekly in our example).

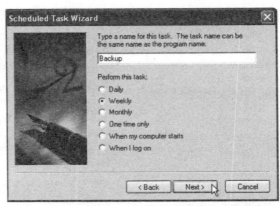

Fig. 27.3 The Third Scheduled Task Wizard Screen.

Having done so, press the **Next** button to display the fourth Wizard screen, shown in Fig. 27.4, where you are asked to specify when you want the selected task to be carried out.

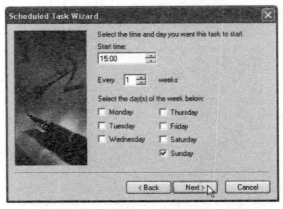

Fig. 27.4 The Fourth Scheduled Task Wizard Screen.

Obviously, your computer must be switched on at the specified day and time. Having done so, press the **Next** button to display the fifth Wizard screen shown in Fig. 27.5 below.

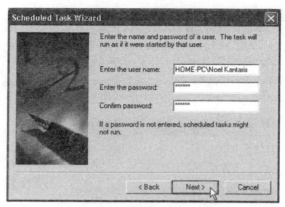

Fig. 27.5 The Fifth Scheduled Task Wizard Screen.

As you can see on the above Wizard screen, you can enter the name of a user and their password. The task is then run as if it were started by the specified user. Clicking **Next**, displays an additional screen (in the case of Backup), shown in Fig. 27.6.

Fig. 27.6 The Sixth Scheduled Backup Wizard Screen.

After providing additional information, click the **OK** button to display the final Wizard screen and clicking the **Finish** button, performs the selected task at its chosen time.

It is a good idea to perform such tasks regularly, but make sure that your computer is switched on at the selected times, and you are not inconvenienced by your time selection. It is, of course, assumed that your PC's clock is set correctly.

The newly created scheduled task now appears in the Scheduled Tasks window, as shown in Fig. 27.7 below.

Fig. 27.7 The Additional Entry in the Scheduled Tasks Window.

To edit a scheduled task, double-click its entry in the above window, which opens the three-tab dialogue box of Fig. 27.6, shown on the previous page, in which you can make changes to the selected Task, its Schedule, and its Settings.

28

Using System Restore

If your PC malfunctions, use System Restore to return your PC to the last date it was working perfectly. Every time you start to install a new program, Windows XP takes a snapshot of your system prior to starting the new installation. Alternatively, you can force Windows to take a snapshot at any time you choose.

To access the System Restore utility, use the *start*, **All Programs, Accessories, System Tools** and click on its icon, shown here, which displays the screen in Fig. 28.1. On this screen you can select to Restore your PC to an earlier time, or create a manual Restore point by clicking the **Create a restore point** option.

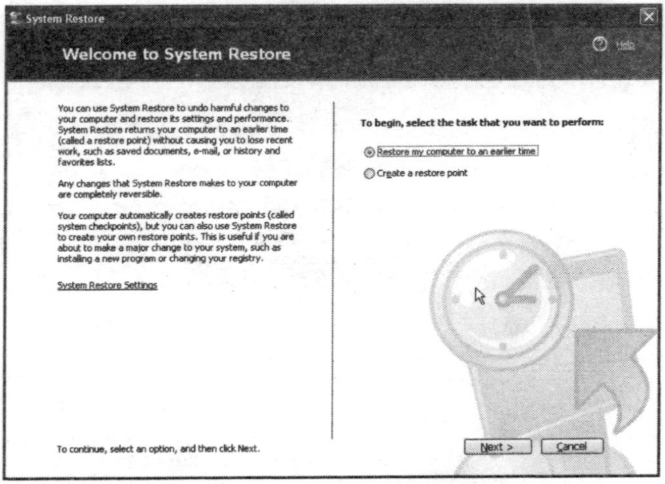

Fig. 28.1 The Welcome to System Restore Screen.

Windows XP asks you to give a description of this Restore point so that you can identify it easily at a later stage.

In our example, shown in Fig. 28.2, we chose to call this **After Installing SP2**, which together with the date given to it by the **Restore** program, will give later a pretty good clue of the circumstances surrounding its creation.

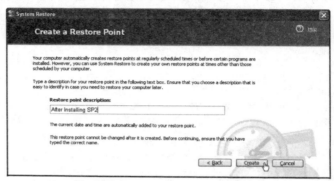

Fig. 28.2 Creating a Manual Restore Point.

Next, activate the **Restore** program, but this time choose the **Restore my computer to an earlier time** option, then click the **Next** button. This displays a further screen, as shown in Fig. 28.3.

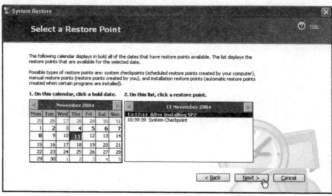

Fig. 28.3 Creating a Manual Restore Point.

The dates shown in bold in the calendar are Restore points created by Windows XP. These could have been created by your computer, manually, or prior to installing certain programs.

29

Using the Windows Update

Update Prior to Service Pack 2

To automatically update Windows System files, if these become available, from Microsoft's Web site, click **start, All Programs**, and select the **Windows Update** menu option.

After connecting to the Internet through your Internet Service Provider (ISP), you will be connected automatically to Microsoft's Web site, as shown in Fig. 29.1 below. If you have installed Service Pack 2, please refer to the next section.

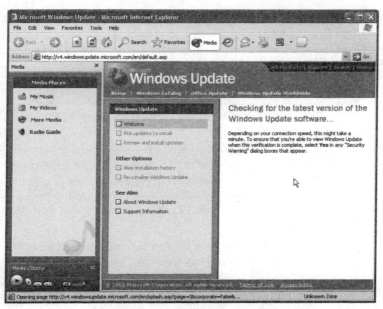

Fig. 29.1 Connecting to Microsoft's Update Home Page.

Next, click the **Welcome** link to get an appropriate list of updates for your system. However, in order to be able to download program patches to your system, the Windows Update program needs to have information relating to your system configuration, as shown in Fig. 29.2.

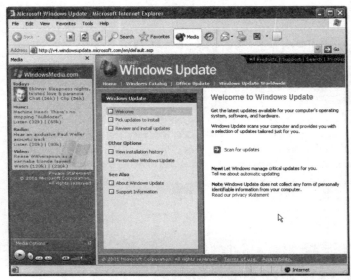

Fig. 29.2 Connecting to Microsoft's Scan for Updates Screen.

Once this is done, you can select which software to download, if any. On successful completion of program downloads, the Windows **Setup** program installs the new patches or programs to your system automatically, after which you can either go back to browse Microsoft's site, or you can disconnect from the Internet.

New to Windows XP is the ability of the program to manage critical updates automatically as you can see on the entry in the right panel of the updates screen. We suggest you spend some time finding out a bit more about this. If you have installed Service Pack 2, Windows will warn you automatically if you do not update often enough as you might be compromising your system's security.

The Windows SP2 Security Center

If you have installed Service Pack 2, you can click the **Security Center** icon in the **Control Panel**, shown here, to display the Windows Security Center screen shown in Fig. 29.3.

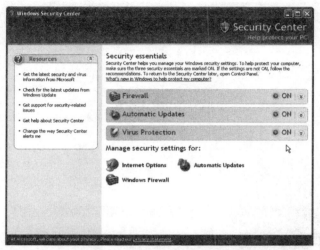

Fig. 29.3 The Windows Security Center Dialogue Box.

The Security Center's job is to make sure that Windows users are kept secure by installing the Firewall, keeping Windows up-to-date at all times, and using antivirus software.

Each of these essential security components has a traffic light indicator; a green light means the security component is in place and is up-to-date, a yellow light indicates that you have disabled its monitor, and a red light means that there is a security risk and you are required to take action.

Each security component can be managed by clicking the relevant link at the bottom of the Security Center screen. We very strongly advise you to use these security components if you want to avoid malicious attacks on your computer from hackers and viruses.

Clicking the **Automatic Update** link on the Windows Security Center screen, displays the screen in Fig. 29.4

Fig. 29.4 The Automatic Updates Dialogue Box.

Note that in this case, Automatic Updates is turned ON by default. From here you can set the day and time for the Automatic Update to be activated.

Alternatively you can click the link pointed to in Fig. 29.4 to connect right now to the Microsoft Update Web site which opens the screen shown in Fig. 29.5 below. The choice is yours.

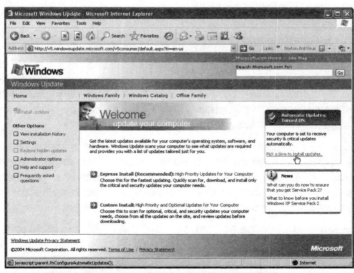

Fig. 29.5 The Windows Update Screen under Service Pack 2.

30

Managing Windows Dual Boot

Installing a Second OS on the Same PC

Suppose you want to install an additional Operating System (OS), say Linux, on your PC which already runs Windows XP. Then before doing so, you need to prepare your system. There are several things you have to do here.

* If Linux is to be installed on a separate, but bootable hard disc, then you don't need any preparation; you can skip the rest of this section.

* If your system has only one hard disc, then you need to consider the following:

  1. If your hard disc is partitioned into, say, a C: and a D: drive, then move all the programs and data you want to retain from drive D: into drive C:, and use the space on drive D: to install Linux as long as there is enough space. Application programs under Windows XP might have to be uninstalled from drive D:, and reinstalled in drive C:.

  2. If your hard disc is not partitioned and you have enough free space at the end of it to load Linux, then use the commercial software package PartitionMagic to create a partition for Linux on your hard disc. Such a program partitions your hard drive without any loss of data.

  3. If you have more than two partitions on your hard drive, none of which is big enough to load Linux, then make a **complete backup** of your hard drive, then use PartitionMagic to rearrange and/or delete such partitions to create a larger partition for Linux.

Changing the Default OS in Dual Boot

To change the default Operating System in a Dual Boot facility, do the following:

- Start by clicking **System** in the Control Panel.

- Next, click the Advanced tab on the displayed System Properties dialogue box to open the screen shown in Fig. 30.1 below.

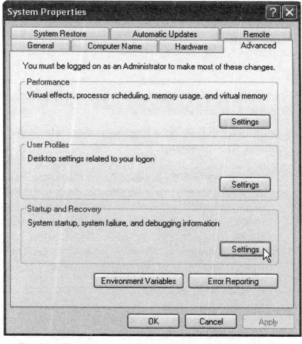

Fig. 30.1 The Advanced System Properties Dialogue Box.

- In this screen, click the **Settings** button, pointed to, under the **Startup and Recovery** option to open the screen shown in Fig. 30.2 on the next page.

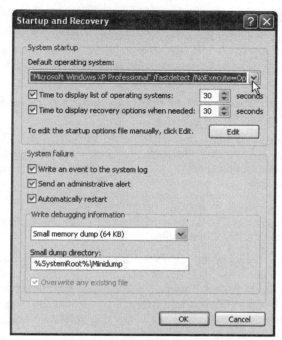

Fig. 30.2 The Startup and Recovery Dialogue Box.

* In Fig. 30.2, click the down-arrow against the **Default operating** system entry and select the Operating System you want to be the default from the drop-down list. On this dialogue box you can also change the time of display of the list of the operating systems.

* Having made the required changes, click the **OK** button so they can take effect.

Removing the Windows Dual Boot

We assume that you have two Operating Systems installed on your computer, say Windows XP and Linux (although the latter could be any previous version of Windows), and you are using the dual boot system to access them.

To remove the second operating system, say Linux in this case, do the following:

- Start by booting the system into Windows XP. Explore your drives and find the one that contains Linux and re-format the entire drive. You may need to confirm your intention.

- Next, select **Run** from the *start* menu, and in the **Open** text box of the displayed dialogue box type **msconfig** and click the **OK** button.

- On the displayed System Configuration Utility dialogue box, click the BOOT.INI tab, and then click the **Check All Boot Paths** button. Your system will report that the path used to launch Linux (the unwanted Operating System) is not valid and offers to remove it. Click the **Yes** button.

From now on, your system will boot directly to Windows XP.

31

Removing Uninstalled Programs

Occasionally you might find that bits of programs are left on your system which the **Add or Remove Programs** application in **Control Panel** is unable to uninstall.

Although information on installed programs, as well as how to remove them, is kept in the Registry, sometimes an error on the program's uninstall configuration can result in bits of the program remaining in the system which might cause the system to become unstable.

To remove all traces of such programs, you need to edit the Registry. However, if you change the Registry without knowing what you are doing, you may well make your computer unusable. Therefore it is important to first make a backup of the Registry key you intend to change, and know how to restore it if things go wrong .

Backing up and Restoring a Registry Key

To export a hive or a single Registry key use the *start*, **Run** command, type **regedit** in the **Open** box of the displayed dialogue box, and click **OK**.

Next, locate and then click the key that contains the value that you want to edit (either an entire hive, as shown in Fig. 31.1 on the next page, or a single key). On the **File** menu of the displayed dialogue box, click **Export**, and in the **Save in** box, select a location where you want to save the Registration Entries. In the **Save as type** drop-down selection box select the **.reg** file type. Finally, in the **File name** box, type a file name, click the **All** radio button, and click **Save**, as shown in Fig. 31.2 also on the next page.

Fig. 31.1 The Restore Wizard Screen.

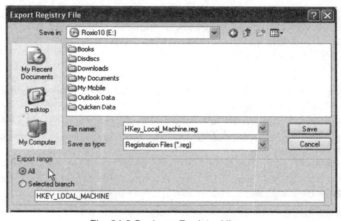

Fig. 31.2 Saving a Registry Hive.

Note the two radio buttons **All** and **Selected branch**. These are used to copy the entire Registry tree, or to copy only the key selected in the Registry and all branches below it, respectively.

The available file types can be seen by clicking the down-arrow to the right of the **Save as type** box, as shown here. The significance of these file types and their use is explained on the next page.

The Registration Files option creates a **.reg** file which can be read and edited either within Notepad as a text file, or directly using the Registry Editor. Once changes have been made and saved within Notepad, right-clicking the file and using the **Merge** command adds the changed file back into the registry. However, any *additions* made to the registry using **regedit** prior to merging, will not be removed.

The Registry Hive Files option creates a binary image of the selected registry key, which cannot be viewed or edited in Notepad or any other text editor. The purpose of such a file is to allow you to import it back into the registry to ensure any problematic changes you made are eliminated.

The Text Files option creates a text file containing the information in the selected key. Its most useful purpose is creating a snapshot of a key that you can refer back to if necessary, but it cannot be merged back into the registry.

The Win9x/NT4 Registration Files option creates a **.reg** file in the same manner used by the Registration Files option. It is only used if you want to merge a key from XP into a previous version of Windows.

Obviously, the most effective and safest method of backing up the registry is to use the Registry Hive Files option. No matter what goes wrong in your editing, importing the image of the key will remove all problematic changes or additions.

A **.reg** file can be restored by navigating to where it is stored, right-clicking it and selecting **Merge** from the drop-down menu. Another option on the same menu is the **Open With** command which displays the Open With dialogue box with the Registry Editor selected. Both these restoring options are also available from the **File** menu when the **.reg** file is selected.

Whichever of the above methods you action, a warning box will be displayed asking you whether you really want the contents of the file to be merged with the equivalent Registry key. The same warning box appears if you double-click the **.reg** file, so take care with your response!

The final method of restoring a **.reg** file is from the Registry Editor menu bar using the **File**, **Import** command, then navigating to where the **.reg** file is saved, selecting the file and clicking **Open**. The contents of the **.reg** file will be merged into the current registry followed by a confirmation dialogue box informing you of the successful outcome! Although this method forces you to consciously select the **.reg** file you want to import, you must be extra careful to select the correct **.reg** file - there is no warning if you don't!

Editing the Registry

To start the editing process, open the Registry, and use the **Edit**, **Find** command and search for the **Uninstall** folder. Press the **F3** function key, until you reach the path:

`HKEY_LOCAL_MACHINE\SOFTWARE\Microsoft\Windows\CurrentVersion\Uninstall`

This sub-folder has entries which appear in the list of the **Add or Remove Programs** application in **Control Panel**. Each entry is displayed as a long name made up of letters and numbers, as shown in the left pane in Fig. 31.3 below.

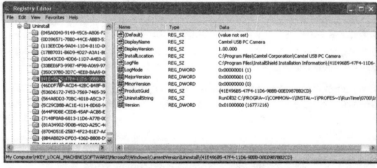

Fig. 31.3 The Contents of the Uninstall Folder.

Highlighting each entry on the left pane displays a list of the program details on the right pane of the Editor. When you find the offending program, simply use the **Ctrl** key to highlight both the Display/Name and the UninstallString keys and press the **Delete** keyboard key.

32

Removing Startup Applications

If you are trying to remove a program and can not find it in the **StartUp** folder, by using the *start*, **All Programs** cascade menu command, then it might be launching itself from the Registry. The Registry keys you will need to examine are:

HKEY_LOCAL_MACHINE\SOFTWARE\Microsoft\Windows\CurrentVersion\Run

HKEY_LOCAL_MACHINE\SOFTWARE\Microsoft\Windows\CurrentVersion\RunOnce

HKEY_LOCAL_MACHINE\SOFTWARE\Microsoft\Windows\CurrentVersion\RunOnceEx

HKEY_CURRENT_USER\Software\Microsoft\Windows\CurrentVersion\Run

However, if you are going to try to change the Registry, we recommended you make backups of your system and the Registry (see previous chapter) before attempting the changes.

To change a Registry key use the *start*, **Run** command, type **regedit** in the **Open** box of the displayed dialogue box, and click **OK**. Next, locate and then click the key that contains the value that you want to edit - for one of our computers, the Registry screen, shown in Fig. 32.1, was displayed as follows.

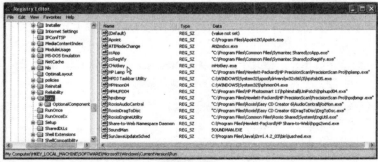

Fig. 32.1 The
HKEY_LOCAL_MACHINE\SOFTWARE\Microsoft\Windows\CurrentVersion\
Run Screen.

On this particular computer the Hotkey application (the one that allows you to configure a button on your keyboard to load a preferred program when pressed), was loading and displaying on the Windows Task bar, thus taking unnecessary space. The offending entry in the Registry is pointed to in Fig. 32.1 and shown magnified below.

To remove it, either highlight the entry and press the **Delete** keyboard key, or double-click the entry and delete the value associated with that application. Whichever method we chose, it solved the problem at hand!

Three additional application entries in Fig. 32.1 were allowed at some time in the past to load on this computer, which now we would like to remove. These are displayed magnified in Fig. 32.2 below.

Share-to-Web Namespace Daemon	REG_SZ	C:\Program Files\Hewlett-Packard\HP Share-to-Web\hpgs2wnd.exe
SoundMan	REG_SZ	SOUNDMAN.EXE
SunJavaUpdateSched	REG_SZ	C:\Program Files\Java\j2re1.4.2_03\bin\jusched.exe

Fig. 32.2 Unwanted programs in HKEY_LOCAL_MACHINE\
SOFTWARE\Microsoft\Windows\CurrentVersion\Run Key.

To remove these from our system, we simply highlighted each in turn and pressed the **Delete** keyboard button. To take effect, such removals require you to restart Windows.

Do remember that with some applications you'll also have to check for entries in the

\SOFTWARE\Microsoft\Windows\CurrentVersion\RunOnce

branch of HKEY_LOCAL_MACHINE, as well as the entries in

\Software\Microsoft\Windows\CurrentVersion\Run

of the HKEY_CURRENT_USER branch.

33

Changing the Registered Owner

When you first used Setup to install Windows XP, you were asked to enter your name and Company name. Like most people we gave our name and typed "Home PC" for the Company name. This information is then assigned by Windows to the Registered Owner of the PC and used by other installed programs for registering purposes. To see this information, use the *start*, **Control Panel** menu command and double-click the **System** icon which displays the System Properties dialogue box with its General tab selected. This screen is shown for one of our computers in Fig. 33.1.

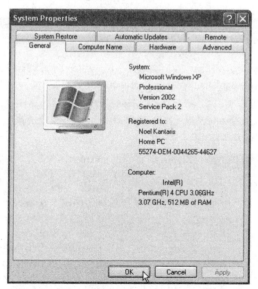

Fig. 33.1 The System Properties Dialogue box.

The Registered owner and Company details, as shown, cannot be changed from within Windows, but you can change them in the Registry. To change the Registered owner and Company name, you need to open the Registry Editor and navigate to:

HKEY_LOCAL_MACHINE\SOFTWARE\Microsoft\Windows NT\CurrentVersion

The values you need to change are **RegisteredOwner** and **RegisteredOrganization**, pointed to in Fig. 33.2.

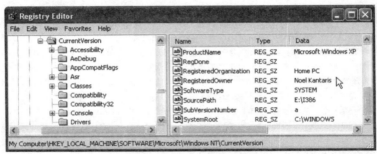

Fig. 33.2 The Registry Editor.

The **CurrentVersion** key, we are interested in here, is to be found in the **Windows NT** branch, although you will find that there is a similarly named key in the **Windows** branch. Both branches are used by Windows XP, with the **Windows NT** branch containing the more advanced settings.

To change a Registry value (make a backup of the Registry key first - see previous chapter), double-click it which opens the Edit String dialogue box shown in Fig. 33.3.

Fig. 33.3 The Edit String Dialogue Box.

You can type what you like in the **Value data** box to replace the current entry. Clicking the **OK** button enters the new value in the Registry. You can repeat this procedure to change the RegisteredOwner value to something else, then open the System Properties dialogue box again, as described earlier, to verify that your changes have taken place.

34

Using the Font Manager

Windows XP uses a Font Manager program to control the installed fonts on your system. You can use the Font Manager to install, view, or delete fonts.

To open the Font Manager, use the *start*, **Control Panel** menu option, and in the displayed screen double-click the **Fonts** icon shown here.

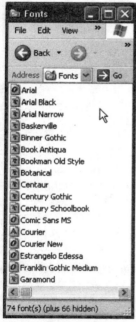

Fig. 34.1 The Fonts Window.

This opens the Fonts window, shown in Fig. 34.1. To control what you see on the Fonts window, click **View** to display the drop-down menu, shown in Fig. 34.2. We have chosen **Status Bar**, **List** and **Hide Variations**.

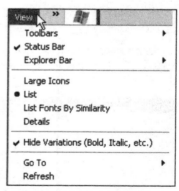

Fig. 34.2 The View Sub-menu.

To see an example of one of the listed fonts, double-click its icon in the Fonts window (Fig. 34.1).

Below we show the Arial (TrueType) font in four different sizes.

Fig. 34.3 Font Size Sample Window for a Selected Font.

You might find it interesting to know, that the Symbol font contains an abundance of Greek letters, while the Webdings and Wingdings Fonts contain special graphic objects.

See page 17 to find out how such characters can be inserted into a document.

New fonts can be installed by selecting the **File, Install New Font** menu command in the Fonts window, as shown in Fig. 34.4. This opens the Add Fonts dialogue box in which you have to specify the disc, folder and file in which the font you want to install resides.

Unwanted fonts can be removed by first highlighting them in the Fonts window, then using the **File, Delete** command. A warning box is displayed.

Fig. 34.4 Installing New Fonts.

35

Creating Private Characters

You can use the Windows Private Character Editor to create your own fonts or logos in Unicode - a 16-bit data encoding system that Windows XP and applications, such as Notepad, WordPad and Microsoft Office, support.

To start the Private Character Editor, use the *start*, **Run** command, type **eudcedit** in the **Open** box of the displayed dialogue box, and click **OK**. This opens a very simple font editor, as shown in Fig. 35.1 below.

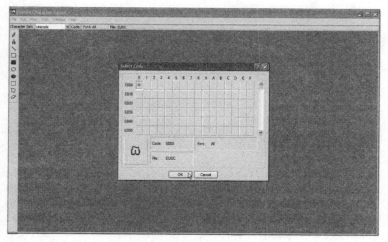

Fig. 35.1 The Opening Screen of the Private Character Editor.

Any characters you have already created are shown with their hexadecimal code (in this case an omega with a tilde on top of it against code E000). You can then click the next code (say E001) that you would like to assigned to your new character. In what follows, we will show you, as an example, how to create the composite of existing characters shown above.

To start the process, click the code E001 on the grid of Fig. 35.1, then click **OK**. This opens the **Edit** screen ready for your drawing. You can use the tools on the left of the screen to fill-in squares on the grid, draw circles, ellipses, squares, rectangles, use the freehand tool, or the eraser. Alternatively, you could use the **Edit**, **Copy Character** menu command to open the screen shown in the composite of Fig. 35.2, where we selected the tilde and clicked the **OK** button, which transfers the selected character to the Edit grid. What is shown below is a composite of the actions you have to take and the result of these actions.

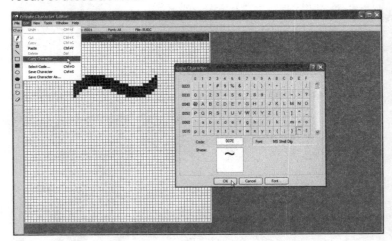

Fig. 35.2 Copying a Character into the Edit Grid Screen.

Next, use the **Window**, **Reference** menu command, as shown in the composite of Fig. 35.3 on the next page, and on the opened Reference screen, scroll down and select the omega character as shown. Clicking the **OK** button, transfers the character of the Reference grid. Again, what is shown in Fig. 35.3 is a composite of the actions you have to take and the result of these actions.

Next, select the omega by right-clicking at one corner outside the character, and with right mouse depressed, drag the mouse pointer to the opposite corner of the character to form an enclosing rectangle, as shown.

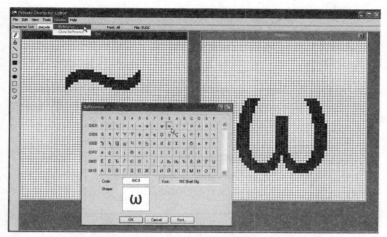

Fig. 35.3 Opening a Character in the Reference Grid Screen.

Releasing the right mouse button, changes the mouse pointer from a cross (right pane) to a four-headed pointer. You can now drag the enclosed omega character from the Reference grid area to the Edit grid area to form the completed character, as shown in the composite of Fig. 35.4.

Fig. 35.4 The Character Construction Process.

Finally, all we have to do is save the constructed character. To do this, use the **File**, **Font Links** menu command to display the Font Links dialogue box, shown in Fig. 35.5, in which you can choose to link this character to all the fonts or to a specific font.

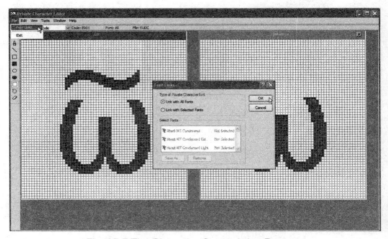

Fig. 35.5 The Character Construction Process.

To use this character, you need to activate the **Character Map** by using the *start*, **All Programs**, **Accessories**, **System Tools** cascade menu command. In the opened Character Map screen, scroll to the **All Fonts (Private Characters)** entry on

Fig. 35.6 The Character Map Screen.

the **Font** list, as shown in Fig. 35.6, click on the character we constructed, then click the **Select** button, followed by the **Copy** button.

Next, open either Notepad, WordPad, or one of the Office applications, and use the **Edit**, **Paste** command to transfer the character into your document.

36

Using Windows ClearType Fonts

Microsoft ClearType is a new development in font display technology that improves font display resolution and hence screen readability. ClearType can improve the resolution of text on colour LCD monitors with a digital interface, such as those in laptops and high-quality flat desktop displays. Readability on CRT screens can also be somewhat improved.

You can turn on ClearType and customise it so it looks best on your screen, either through an online Web-interface, or by downloading the ClearType Tuner PowerToy from Microsoft which lets you activate and tune your ClearType settings via the Windows **Control Panel**.

The online tuner can be found at:

  http://www.microsoft.com/typography/ClearType/tuner/1.htm

while the ClearType Tuner PowerToy can be downloaded from Microsoft's site by starting Internet Explorer, typing the address:

  http://www.microsoft.com/typography/ClearTypePowerToy.mspx

and clicking the **Go** button. Part of what displays on your screen is shown in Fig. 36.1 on the next page. The Web page explains what ClearType fonts are, and a lot more besides.

To download the ClearType Tuner PowerToy, click the link

  Http://download.microsoft.com

pointed to in Fig. 36.1, which opens the dialogue box shown in Fig. 36.2, also on the next page.

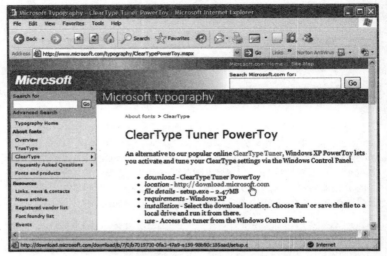

Fig. 36.1 The Microsoft Typography Web Page.

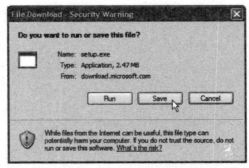

Fig. 36.2 The File Download Security Warning Box.

We suggest you save the downloaded file in a convenient folder (we created a folder in the C: drive and named it **Downloads**) and after the download is completed, click the **Run** button on the displayed dialogue box. After installation you will be able to tune your display to its best resolution. After restarting your computer you will find an additional icon in **Control Panel**, as shown here which can be used later to change the selected settings.

37

Displaying Windows in Full Screen

Whether you display a window using **My Computer**, **Windows Explorer**, or **Internet Explorer** you can use the **F11** function key to substantially increase the visible area, as shown in Fig. 37.1.

Fig. 37.1 Displaying an Explorer Window in Full View.

Note that by default, the Explorer toolbar at the top of the screen with the standard buttons, shown in Fig. 37.2, remains visible, together with the **Minimise**, **Restore**, and **Close** buttons at the top right corner of the screen - these three buttons only display if Service Pack 2 is installed. The displayed visible area of such a window, extends over the *start* button and the Task bar.

If you want to reclaim the area occupied by the Explorer toolbar as well, right-click the toolbar and select **Auto-Hide** from the drop-down menu. Clicking anywhere in the main window causes the toolbar to disappear. To make it reappear, move the mouse to the top of the window. To make the *start* button and Task bar appear, move the mouse to the bottom of the window.

Fig. 37.2 The Right-click Explorer Toolbar Menu.

Pressing **F11** again will return Windows Explorer to normal view. If this does not work, click the **Restore** button shown at the right of the screen in Fig. 37.2. If you do not have Service Pack 2 installed, and pressing the **F11** function key does not restore the window, then use the **Alt+Space bar** key combination to open the menu shown in Fig. 37.3. From here you **Restore**, **Minimize**, or **Close** the expanded Explorter window.

Fig. 37.3 The Alt+Space bar menu.

As you can see, with Service Pack 2 installed, you can use the **F11** function key to toggle between full screen and its previous size screen, whether the latter was a maximised screen or not. Perhaps another good reason to install SP2.

ment>

38

Managing Internet Options

Click the **Internet Options** icon in the **Control Panel**, shown here, to open the dialogue box in Fig. 38.1.

Fig. 38.1 The Internet Properties Dialogue Box.

In the General tab sheet, you can specify which page to use for your Home page (the one that is displayed when you first open Internet Explorer). You could, for example use your own Web site, or one of the Web search engines, such as google.com, or any other Web site.

From this tab sheet, you can also **Delete Cookies**, which is information created and stored on your hard disc by Web sites you visited. Furthermore, you can also **Delete Files** which are temporary Internet files holding information on pages you visited before on a Web site. These files allow you to browse quickly through such pages because your Internet browser checks and uses them (if the information in them has not changed) in preference to downloading them from the Internet, which takes much longer.

Fig. 38.2 The Settings Dialogue Box.

Obviously such temporary Internet files can take a lot of hard disc space, but you can control this by clicking the **Settings** button to open the dialogue box shown in Fig. 38.2. In here you can select from several options for checking for newer versions of stored Web pages, and you can limit the amount of hard disc space used by them. Click the **View Files** button to see a list of the temporary files held on your computer. Occasionally you might need to delete such temporary files, particularly if the space allocated for them is full, as it might have ramifications in other areas - see next chapter.

Going back to the General tab sheet of the Internet Properties dialogue box, you will see options at the bottom of the box dealing with **History**. This is a folder that holds links to pages you have visited, for quick access to recently viewed Web site pages without having to connect to the Internet.

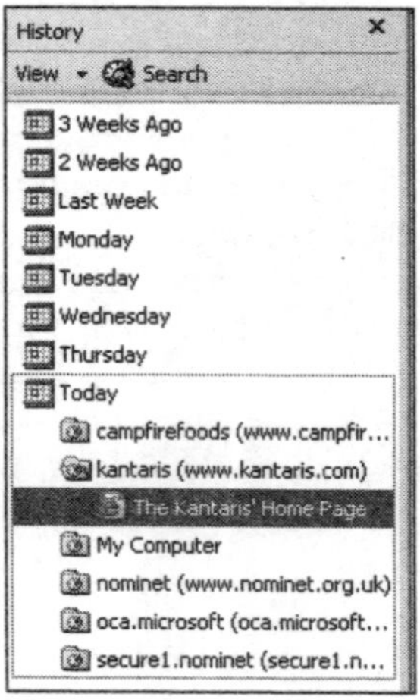

To view history links, click the **History** Toolbar button, shown here to the right, on a Windows XP application such as the **Internet Explorer** or **My Computer** (to do this, use the **View**, **Toolbars**, **Customize** menu command), to open the History panel, shown in Fig. 38.3. You can choose History links from **Today** to several **Weeks Ago**.

Fig. 38.3 The History Panel.

Internet Security

If you want to stop people getting at your data or tracking what you are doing, then Internet security is important to you.

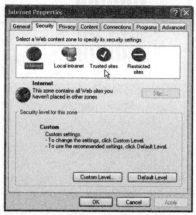

Fig. 38.4 The Internet Security Screen.

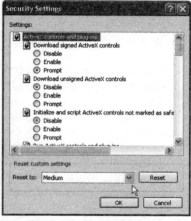

Fig. 38.5 The Security Settings Screen.

Clicking the Security tab of the Internet Properties dialogue box displays the sheet shown in Fig. 38.4. As each item under **Select a Web content zone to specify its security settings** at the top of the screen is selected, its security settings are shown below the selection area. For example, when **Internet** is selected, you are told that 'This zone contains all Web sites you haven't placed in other zones'. To change the settings, click the **Custom Level** button to display the Security Settings dialogue box shown in Fig. 38.5. In this screen you can select settings for various **ActiveX controls**. These are potentially risky actions, with some of the options not providing a **Prompt** setting.

None of these options apply to FTP folders, which are folders you upload or download to or from Web sites using the File Transfer Protocol which, however, does not use encryption or other security mechanism to protect your password when you log on to a server.

Internet Privacy

Clicking the Privacy tab of the Internet Properties dialogue box displays the screen in Fig. 38.6. Here you can specify the

Fig. 38.6 The Internet Privacy Screen.

security level for the Internet zone. As you move the slide up a notch at a time, you impose higher and higher security, while moving the slide downwards diminishes it. An explanation on what is allowed and what is not, is given next to the slide as you move it to a different level. You can also override cookie handling for individual Web sites by clicking **Edit** and filling in the displayed sheet.

Fig. 38.7 The Advanced Privacy Settings Screen.

Clicking the **Advanced** button, displays the screen shown in Fig. 38.7, in which you can control cookies. If the override box (pointed to) is not checked, the options under it are greyed out. In that case, the Web site's privacy policy, if it exists, is displayed by **Internet Explorer**, which tells you what kind of information the Web site collects, and how it uses it. Also, Web sites might provide a (P3P) (Platform for Privacy Preferences Policy), in which case **Internet Explorer** might be able to compare your privacy settings to that of the P3P privacy policy, and determine whether or not to allow the Web site to save cookies on your PC. If you check the override box, then you must decide how first-party and third-party cookies should be treated.

Internet Content

Clicking the Content tab of the Internet Properties dialogue box

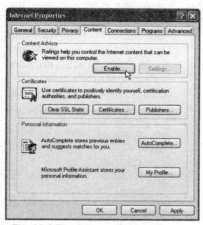

Fig. 38.8 The Internet Content Screen.

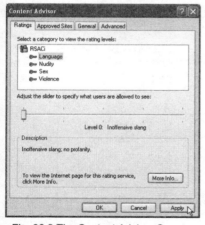

Fig. 38.9 The Content Advisor Screen.

displays the screen in Fig. 38.8. The most important option on this screen is the **Content Advisor** which helps you to control the Internet content that can be viewed on your computer. Clicking the **Enable** button displays the screen shown in Fig. 38.9, where you can set ratings on Language, Nudity, Sex, and Violence permitted to be viewed.

You set these ratings by selecting each option and moving the slide to the right a notch at a time, which lowers the level of restriction. What is allowed to be viewed is displayed in the **Description** box as you move the slide. Once you have set ratings to all the listed options, click the **Apply** button followed by **OK**. This displays the Create Supervisor Password dialogue box so that you can protect these ratings.

Other options on the Content tab screen, allow you to use **Certificates** to identify yourself, change the **AutoComplete** settings, or specify **Personal information** you can share when a Web site requests information from its visitors.

Internet Connection

Clicking the Connections tab of the Internet Properties

dialogue box displays the screen in Fig. 38.10. Under the **Dial-up and Virtual Private Network settings** you will see a list of our Internet connections which are already available on this computer.

To set up a new Internet connection, click the **Setup** button which starts the **New Connection Wizard** shown in Fig. 38.11.

Fig. 38.10 The Internet Connections Tab-sheet.

As you can see, this Wizard can be used to connect to the Internet or a private network, or set up a home or small office network.

Fig. 38.11 The New Connection Wizard.

To continue, click **Next** and follow the instructions on the screen.

Using a Broadband Connection

To use broadband, you must first select a Broadband ISP. A quick search on the Internet (try www.google.com) will unveil the most current offers, but before choosing, look at pricing and restrictions associated with particular connections. Look out for the following points:

*   Do they charge you a connection/installation fee.

*   Do they provide you with a free broadband modem - see next page for choice of available modems, which are dependant on the type of connection required.

*   What are the monthly connection fees. These depend on a choice of connection speeds which can vary from 5 times to 15 times the speed of a dial-up (56 Kbps) modem, the most typical one being 10 times (512 Kbps) for domestic use.

*   Does the pricing include the availability of e-mail addresses, mail filtering, and Web site hosting.

*   What restrictions are included in the pricing - some providers only allow a certain amount of Internet brows-ing a month, others do not allow you to play games on-line, while others only allow one computer to be connected to the Internet.

Next, find out whether your premises are near enough to the exchange and whether broadband is available at that particular exchange. Both of these requirements can be found out quickly and easily by simply selecting the appropriate option on your chosen ISP's Web site, and typing in your postcode.

If all is well, you can now select the type of broadband modem you require. Broadly speaking, there are three types of modems you might want to use as a domestic user. These are:

1) A simple broadband modem which connects to your computer's USB port. This is the type most commonly provided free by ISPs and can only connect a single computer.

2) A broadband modem that provides both a USB and an Ethernet (LAN) connection. This type can use either connection for broadband, or use the LAN port to connect two computers together and the USB port to connect to broadband.

3) A four-port Ethernet (LAN) broadband router that uses one of the ports for broadband connection and the other ports for networking additional computers.

The above broadband modems are usually referred to as ADSL (Asymmetric Digital Subscriber Line) modems. Such modems allow high-speed connection to the Internet and also voice transmissions over the same telephone line. ADSL modems can be of the wired type or wireless type, with the latter being more expensive.

Other types of high-speed services which you might have come across are:

- ISDN (Integrated Services Digital Network) - a high-speed digital telephone service than enables connection to the Internet with a speed of 128 Kbps.

- Cable connection requiring a cable modem - a device that enables a broadband connection to the Internet by using cable television infrastructure with access speeds of as much as 10 Mbps.

- DSL (Digital Subscriber Line) - similar to ADSL. DSL modems can be internal or external. Internal DSL modems are plugged into an expansion slot in the computer and do not require a network adapter. External DSL modems use a network adapter to connect to the computer, therefore your PC must be network ready.

Returning to the ADSL broadband connection, you should be aware of additional limitations which may not come to light until well after you have signed up with a provider and were given or bought a modem.

For example, you need to be aware of the following facts:

If the distance between the main BT socket into your house and the extension where your computer is connected, is greater than 10 metres, a USB connection to the broadband modem may not work - there will not be a strong enough signal for synchronisation. In that case, a broadband modem with an Ethernet connection might solve the problem, but the type 1 modem, as specified on the previous page (sometimes given to you free by your broadband supplier), may not be of much use.

If you bought a type 2 modem, as specified on the previous page, with one USB and one Ethernet connection port and you had to use the Ethernet port to connect to the broadband modem because of signal synchronisation problems, then you can not connect anything else to the Internet unless you also buy an Ethernet hub.

Therefore, it might be a good idea to research broadband modems before you commit yourself to any specific type. Try to select one with a built-in firewall. It is also vital to find out if technical support is charged as extra. Some ISPs can charge as much as £1.50 per minute!

Installing a Broadband Modem

In what follows, we assume that you connected your modem to your PC via the USB port, being the most common connection.

As most installations are Plug-and-Play, Windows XP automatically detects the modem and the message 'Found New Hardware' is displayed at the bottom right corner of your screen. The **Found New Hardware Wizard** then starts which guides you through the installation procedure. The same Wizard can be started manually, by clicking the **Add Hardware** icon in **Control Panel**, shown here.

If the modem is not recognised immediately by Windows, insert the manufacturer's CD in the CD-ROM drive and make sure the Wizard looks for the drivers on that drive. The next Wizard screen should then notify you that the USB drivers have been found and clicking **Next** proceeds with the transfer of the drivers to your hard disc.

Optionally you can connect another computer using its Ethernet port, before going on to configure your connection.

Configuring a Broadband Connection

In what follows, we assume that you have connected your broadband modem to your computer via the USB port, and that

Internet Options

the required drivers for the modem for this type of connection have been installed. Having done so, click the **Internet Options** icon in **Control Panel**, shown here, then click the Connections tab of the displayed Internet Properties dialogue box to open the window in Fig. 39.1.

To set up a new Internet connection, click the **Setup** button which displays the Welcome screen of the **New Connection Wizard**, and follow the instructions on the screen.

Fig. 39.1 The Internet Connections Tab-sheet.

40

Saving Web Pictures

The following problem can arise if you are using Microsoft Internet Explorer 6.0 Service Pack 1, with Microsoft Windows XP Home Edition.

While browsing the Internet, you might find an image that you would like to save a copy of, so you right-click it and select the **Save Picture As** option from the drop-down menu, as shown in Fig. 40.1.

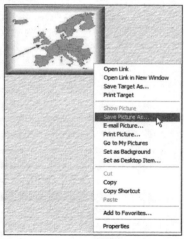

In the displayed Save Picture dialogue box, you may find that you are unable to save the file to its original filename extension (such as GIF or JPEG), and the only image format offered is that of .bmp. The reason for this might be:

(a) The Temporary Internet cache on your PC is full. To delete such temporary files, use the *start*, **Control Panel** menu command and click the **Internet Options** icon shown here. In the General tab sheet of the displayed dialogue box click the **Delete**

Fig. 40.1 The Save Picture As Option.

Files button - see the previous chapter.

(b) You may have the option **Do not save encrypted pages to disk** selected in the Advanced Tab sheet of the Internet Options dialogue box under the **Security** section and are loading the page over a secure connection (https).

To solve the problem, click the **Do not save encrypted pages to disk** to remove the check mark, then click the **Apply** button, as shown in Fig. 40.2.

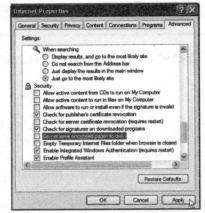

Fig. 40.2 The Advanced Tab Sheet of the Internet Properties Screen.

System and Explorer Versions

To find out which Service Pack of the Operating System you are running, use the *start*, **Control Panel** menu command and in the displayed window double-click the **System** icon shown here. This opens the System Properties dialogue box and on the General tab screen you will find information relating to your system, as shown in Fig. 40.3.

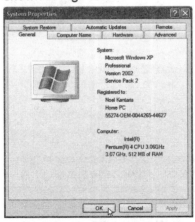

Fig. 40.3 The System Properties Screen.

To find out which version of Internet explorer you are using, activate the program and use the **Help, About Internet Explorer** menu option to open the screen shown in Fig. 40.4 below.

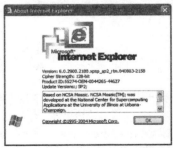

Fig. 40.4 The About Internet Explorer Screen.

41

Saving a Desktop Image

Apart from cutting, copying and pasting operations in Windows applications, you can also use the Clipboard to copy the contents of an application's window, or to copy Windows graphics images, so that you can transfer such information to other applications. There are two ways of copying information:

- Press the **Print Screen** key (usually found to the right of the **F12** function key) to copy onto the Clipboard the contents of a whole Windows screen, even if that screen is a DOS application.

- Press the **Alt+Print Screen** key combination to copy onto the Clipboard the contents of the current open window, or dialogue box.

To illustrate these techniques follow the step-by-step instructions given below.

Copying a Full Windows Screen

Use the *start*, **Control Panel** menu command, then

- Move the **Control Panel** displayed window next to the Recycle Bin but without obscuring its icon on the desktop.

- Press the **Print Screen** key, then activate **Paint** using the *start*, **All Programs**, **Accessories**, menu command, then select the **Paint** option, shown here, and finally use the **Edit**, **Paste** menu command on the displayed screen.

What now appears on the **Paint** screen, or something like it, is shown in Fig. 41.1 on the next page.

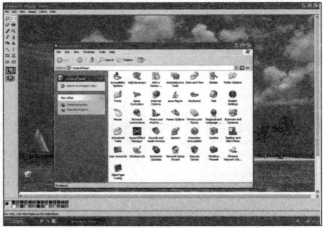

Fig. 41.1 The Contents of the Clipboard.

Copying the Contents of a Current Open Window

Open **Control Panel**, then

- Press the **Alt+Print Screen** key, then activate **Paint**, then use the **Edit, Paste** menu command. What is displayed now is the current window only.

Copying a DOS Screen

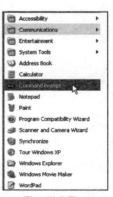

Use the **start**, **All Programs**, **Accessories** menu command, then

- Click the **Command Prompt** option on the cascade menu shown in Fig. 41.2.

- Start your DOS application, then continue as above.

DOS applications can run in a window or in full screen. You can switch from one to the other by pressing **Alt+Enter**.

Fig. 41.2 The Accessories Menu.

42

Using the On-Screen Keyboard

To activate the On-Screen Keyboard, use the *start*, **Run** menu command, then type **osk** in the **Open** box of the Run box, as shown in Fig. 42.1 below.

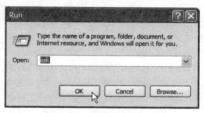

Fig. 42.1 The Run Dialogue Box.

This displays the screen shown in Fig. 42.2 below. The virtual keyboard allows users with either mobility impairments, or users of a tablet PC, to type data using a pointing device or joystick. The result is exactly as if you were using the actual keyboard.

Fig. 42.2 The On-Screen Virtual Keyboard.

The On-Screen Keyboard has three typing modes you can use to type data. These are:

Clicking mode - you click the on-screen keys to type text.

Hovering mode - you use a mouse or joystick to point to a key for a predefined period of time, and the selected character is typed automatically.

Scanning mode - the On-screen keyboard continually scans the keyboard and highlights areas where you can type keyboard characters by pressing a hot key or using a switch-input device.

Fig. 42.3 The Settings Menu of the On-Screen Keyboard.

The three typing modes are selected by choosing the **Settings Typing Mode** menu command, as shown in Fig. 42.3. This opens the Typing Mode dialogue box (Fig. 42.4) in which you click the option you prefer and, if appropriate, the time interval before the command is actioned.

Also, you can select from the **Settings** menu to have the virtual keyboard appear **Always on Top** of all other windows displayed on your screen, and select to **Use Click Sound** which is useful if you are using the **Hovering** option of typing.

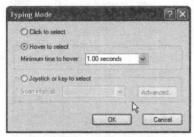

Fig. 42.4 The Typing Mode of the On-Screen Keyboard.

Fig. 42.5 The Keyboard Menu of the On-Screen Keyboard.

There are several types of On-Screen Keyboards which are chosen from the **Keyboard** menu (Fig. 42.5). These are the **Enhanced Keyboard** that includes the numeric keypad, and the **Standard Keyboard** that does not include the numeric keypad.

You can also display the keyboard with the keys in the **Regular Layout**, or in a **Block Layout** (arranged in rectangular blocks). Block layout is especially useful in scanning mode. Finally, you can select to display the US standard keyboard (**101 keys**), the universal keyboard (**102 keys**), or a Japanese characters keyboard (**106 keys**).

43

Using the Microsoft Magnifier

To activate the Microsoft Magnifier, use the *start*, **Run** menu command, then type **magnify** in the **Open** box of the Run box, as shown in Fig. 43.1 below.

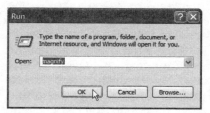

Fig. 43.1 The Run Dialogue Box.

The displayed Magnifier screen is shown in Fig. 43.2 below. The display of the Microsoft Magnifier message can be prevented from displaying by clicking the **Do not show this message again** box.

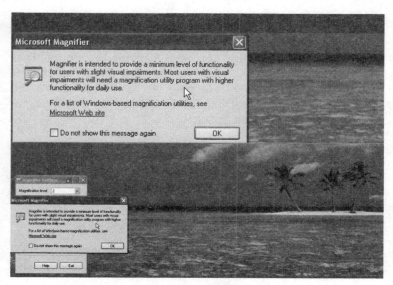

Fig. 43.2 The Magnifier Screen.

However, before closing this message, note that it is magnified at the top of the screen, as shown in Fig. 43.2, because the mouse pointer happens to be within the actual (lower) message box.

In fact, wherever you move the mouse pointer, that part of the screen is magnified in a window at the top of the screen. The magnifying window can be made bigger in the usual way, by dragging one side in the direction you want to increase its size.

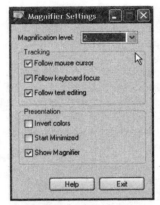

Fig. 43.3 The General Magnifier Settings Box.

After closing the Microsoft Magnifier message box, the Magnifier Settings dialogue box becomes fully visible, as shown in Fig. 43.3. From here you can set the **Magnification level** from 1 (low) to 9 (high), and select **Tracking** and **Presentation** options. Clicking the **Exit** button removes the Magnifier facility from your screen.

Selecting **Start Minimized** under **Presentation**, minimises the Magnifier Settings box on the Task bar next time you start the Magnifier. To now exit the Magnifier, click the Magnifier Settings entry on the Task bar and remove the minimise option.

44

Controlling the Mouse

To adjust or troubleshoot your mouse, click the **Mouse** button, shown here, in the **Control Panel**, to open the multi-tab Mouse Properties dialogue box shown in Fig. 44.1.

Use the Buttons tab screen to switch primary and secondary buttons, depending on whether you are right- or left-handed, adjust the amount of time between clicks when you double-click the primary mouse button, or lock the primary button after a single click, so that you can select or drag items without having to continuously hold down the mouse button. Click again to release ClickLock. To change the time interval before ClickLock takes effect, click the **Settings** button.

Fig. 44 .1 The Mouse Properties Screen.

Mouse Pointer Options

Use the Pointers tab screen to see the default set of pointers used by the system to indicate what action is being carried out at any given moment. You can even build your own set of pointers by using the **Browse** button on the sheet to display and choose from the alternative pointers held in the **Cursors** folder.

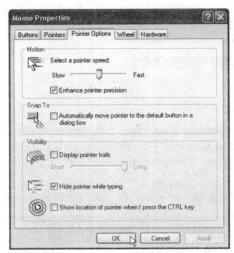

Fig. 44.2 The Mouse Pointer Options Screen.

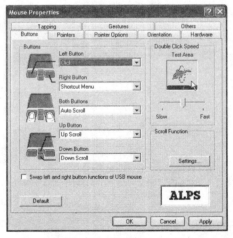

Fig. 44.3 The Mouse Properties Screen.

The Pointer Options tab screen (Fig. 44.2), makes it easier to work with the mouse. For example, you can adjust the distance that the pointer moves with respect to the distance covered by the mouse; you can automatically make the pointer snap to the default button in a dialogue box; you can add a trail to the mouse pointer to make it more visible; or you can show the location of the mouse pointer when you press the **Ctrl** key.

If you are using a laptop computer, you will most likely be using its touch pad. In that case, clicking the **Mouse** button on the **Control Panel**, displays the screen in Fig. 44.3 in place of the screen Fig. 44.1.

Most of the options on this dialogue box are self-explanatory and similar to those shown in Fig. 44.1 as already discussed. In this particular Mouse Properties dialogue box, there is even a test area for you to practice double-clicking which displays the animated imagery pointed to in Fig. 44.3.

45

Using the Address Book

The Address Book can be used not only with the Fax utility, but
also with Outlook Express (the E-mail utility that comes with
Windows XP). Although Fax numbers are straightforward to
deal with, e-mail addresses are often quite complicated and
not at all easy to remember. Windows provides an Address
Book in which Fax numbers, telephone numbers, and e-mail
addresses can be gathered together and used by its various
communication utilities.

To access the Address Book, use the *start*, **All Programs**,
Accessories menu command, and select the
Address Book option. In Fig. 45.1 below, we show
part of an example.

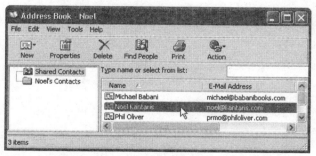

Fig. 45.1 The Address Book Screen.

Once in the Address Book, you can manually
add a person's details, Fax number and e-mail
address, in the Properties box that opens when
you click the **New** toolbar icon and select **New
Contact**, as shown here. Selecting **New Group**
from this drop-down menu lets you create a grouping of e-mail
addresses, you can then send a Fax or an e-mail to everyone
in the group with one operation.

The **New Contact** button lets you add details for a new person to the Address Book, and the **Properties** button lets you edit an existing entry, as shown in Fig. 45.2 below.

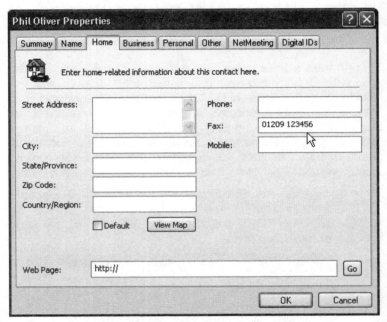

Fig. 45.2 A Recipient's Properties Screen.

The Home tab screen is used to enter the recipient's address, telephone and Fax number. You can also enter similar information for Businesses. Use the Name tab to enter the name, title, and e-mail address for the recipient. Transferring information about your contacts (at this stage, name, Fax number, and e-mail address) will save you a lot of time in the future. The rest of the information pertaining to an individual can be entered later as it is needed, by editing an Address Book entry.

46

E-mail with Outlook Express

To use Outlook Express 6 (the e-mail and news facility program) built into Windows XP, left-click the **Outlook Express** menu option on the *start* menu, shown here. The program should already have been added to your PC by **Setup**. If you can't find it there, use the *start*, **All Programs**, **Outlook Express** menu option. Some users might prefer to have a shortcut to Outlook Express on their desktop (right-click it and use the **Send To, Desktop** command), while others might prefer to have it placed in the Quick Launch area of the Task bar (drag it there). The choice is yours!

Clicking any of these actions opens Outlook Express and displays the screen shown in Fig. 46.1 below.

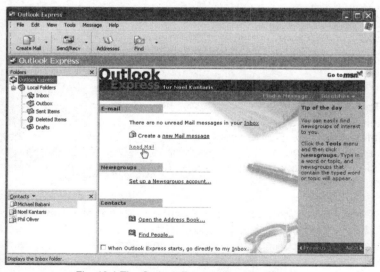

Fig. 46.1 The Outlook Express Opening Screen.

Obviously, to send and receive electronic mail over a modem, you must make an arrangement with a commercial server. Once you have registered with such a service, you will be provided with all the necessary information to enter in the Internet Connection Wizard, so that you can fully exploit all the available facilities.

Connecting to your Server

To tell Outlook Express how to connect to your server's facilities, you must complete your personal e-mail connection details in the Internet Connection Wizard, which opens when you first attempt to use the Read Mail facility pointed to in Fig. 46.1.

If the Wizard does not open, or if you want to change your connection details, use the **Tools**, **Accounts** menu command, select the mail tab and click the **Add** button and select **Mail**, as shown in the composite screen in Fig. 46.2 below.

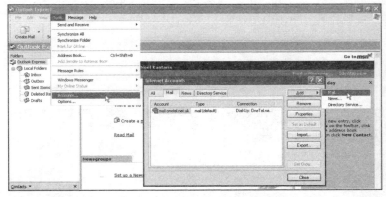

Fig. 46.2 The Internet Accounts Options Screen of Outlook Express.

Once your connection is established, you can click the **Read Mail** coloured link, or the **Inbox** entry in the Folder List to read your mail. Opening the **Inbox** for the first time, will probably display a message from Microsoft, like that shown in Fig. 46.3 on the next page.

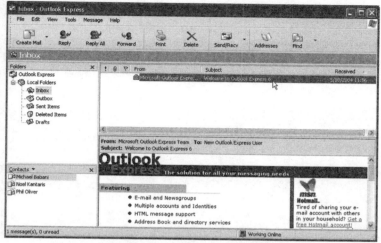

Fig. 46.3 The Inbox Outlook Express Screen.

This shows the default Outlook Express Main window layout, which consists of a **Folders List** to the left with a **Contacts** list (from the Address Book) below it, a Message List to the right and a Preview Pane below that. The list under **Folders** contains all the active mail folders, news servers and newsgroups. Clicking on one of these displays its contents in the **Message List**. Clicking on a message opens a Preview of it, while double-clicking on a message opens the message in its own window.

The Message List

When you select a folder, by clicking it in the Folders list, the Message list shows the contents of that folder. Brief details of each message are displayed on one line, as shown in Fig. 46.4.

Fig. 46.4 Received Messages in Ascending Date Order.

The first column shows the message priority, if any, the second whether the message has an attachment, and the third whether the message has been 'flagged'. All of these are indicated by icons on the message line, a list of which is shown in Fig. 46.5 below.

The Message Status Icons

The message status icons together with their meaning are listed below.

This icon	Indicates this
	The message has one or more files attached.
!	The message has been marked high priority by the sender.
↓	The message has been marked low priority by the sender.
	The message has been read. The message heading appears in light type.
	The message has not been read. The message heading appears in bold type.
	The message has been replied to.
	The message has been forwarded.
	The message is in progress in the Drafts folder.
	The message is digitally signed and unopened.
	The message is encrypted and unopened.
	The message is digitally signed, encrypted and unopened.
	The message is digitally signed and has been opened.
	The message is encrypted and has been opened.
	The message is digitally signed and encrypted, and has been opened.
⊞	The message has responses that are collapsed. Click the icon to show all the responses (expand the conversation).
⊟	The message and all of its responses are expanded. Click the icon to hide all the responses (collapse the conversation).
	The unread message header is on an IMAP server.
	The opened message is marked for deletion on an IMAP server.
	The message is flagged.
	The IMAP message is marked to be downloaded.
	The IMAP message and all conversations are marked to be downloaded.
	The individual IMAP message (without conversations) is marked to be downloaded.

Fig. 46.5. Table of Message Status Icons.

Of these, the most important, for most users, is the one that indicates tnat the message has one or more files attached.

47

Using E-mail Attachments

If you want to include an attachment to your main e-mail message, you simply click the **Attach** toolbar button in the New Message window, as shown in Fig. 47.1 below.

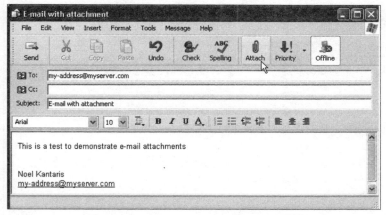

Fig. 47.1 Adding an Attachment to an E-mail.

This opens the Insert Attachment dialogue box, shown in Fig. 47.2 on the next page, for you to select the file, or files, you want to go with your message.

In Outlook Express the attached files are placed below the **Subject** text box. In Fig. 47.3, also displayed on the next page, we show two attachments with their distinctive icons that tell the recipient what each file is; a Word (**.doc**) document file and a graphics (**.jpg**) file in this case.

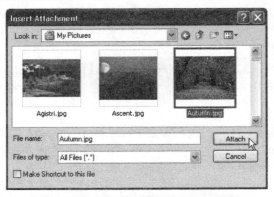

Fig. 47.2 The Insert Attachment Dialogue Box.

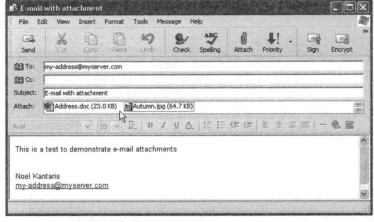

Fig. 47.3 Adding an Attachment to an E-mail.

It is only polite to include in your e-mail a short description of what the attachments are, and which applications were used to create them; it will help the recipient to decipher them.

Clicking the **Send** icon on the toolbar, shown here, puts each e-mail (with its attachments, if any) in Outlook's **Outbox** folder. Next time you click the **Send/Recv** toolbar icon, Outlook Express connects to your ISP (Internet Service Provider) and sends all the e-mails stored in it.

Receiving E-mail Attachments

To demonstrate what happens when you receive an e-mail with attachments, we have sent the above e-mail to ourselves, then a minute or so later we received it back, as shown in Fig. 47.4 below. This is a good way of testing your e-mail settings.

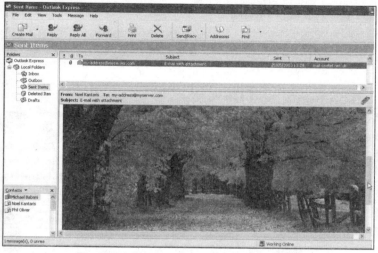

Fig. 47.4 A Received E-mail with Attachments.

Fig. 47.5 E-mail Attachments.

Note that the received e-mail shows the graphics (**.jpg**) file open at the bottom of the Preview pane, but there is no indication of any other attachments. To find out how many attachments were included with the received e-mail, left-click the Attach (paper clip) icon pointed to in Fig. 47.5 to display all of them.

Left-clicking a graphics (.jpg) file opens it in the Photo Editor, while left-clicking the document file opens the Warning box shown in Fig. 47.6. Each attached file can be opened in situ or saved to disc by selecting **Open it** or **Save it to disk**.

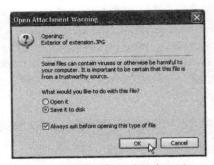

Fig. 47.6 The Open Attachment Warning Window.

Attachments and Security

Most viruses are usually associated with attachments. Therefore, the first golden rule is "never open an attachment unless you know the sender". The second rule is to switch on the extensions of known file types so you can see the true extension of attachments. To do this, use **My Computer**, select **Tools, Folder Options** on the menu bar of the displayed window, click the **View** tab, and remove the check mark from

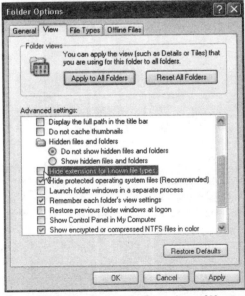

Fig. 47.7 Making Visible the Extensions of Known File Types.

the **Hide extensions of known file types** box, pointed to in Fig. 47.7 with its View tab selected.

48

Controlling E-mail Connection

If you have a modem connection to the Internet, it can be annoying when Outlook Express goes into dial-up mode when you start the program. To change the program settings, start the program, then open the **Tools**, **Options**, Connection tabbed sheet, shown in Fig. 48.1 below.

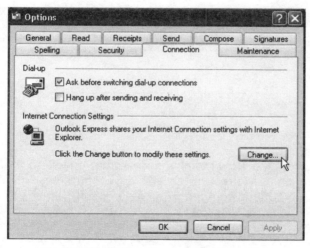

Fig. 48.1 The Options Connection Dialogue Box.

This gives you some control of what happens when you open Outlook Express, depending on your connection settings for Internet Explorer. To look at these settings, click the **Change** button which displays the dialogue box in Fig. 48.2 shown on the next page.

Fig. 48.2 The Internet Properties Dialogue Box.

Next, select the **Never dial a connection** option so that you only 'go on line' (as long as you have not chosen to **Work Offline** from the **File** menu option), when you click the **Send/Recv** toolbar icon shown here. If you have more than one Internet connection, the down arrow to the right of the icon lets you select which one to use.

If, on the other hand, you have a permanent Internet connection, like broadband, you might like to deselect the **Never dial a connection** option.

49

Using Phone & Modem Options

Double-clicking the **Phone and Modem Options** icon in the **Control Panel**, shown here, displays the three-tab screen shown in Fig. 49.1 below.

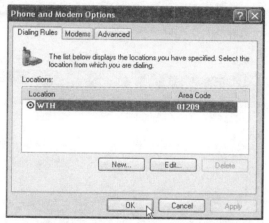

Fig. 49.1 The Phone and Modem Options Screen.

Use these tabbed sheets to add new dialling locations to your computer, or edit existing dialling locations; install a new modem or display and change information about a selected modem; display or configure installed telephony providers on your computer, add to the list, or remove from the list.

Before using your modem, check to ensure it is configured correctly. To do this, click the Modems tab (Fig. 49.1), then in the displayed dialogue box, shown in Fig. 49.2 on the next page, click the **Properties** button, which opens the Properties dialogue box for the installed modem.

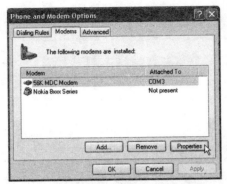

Fig. 49.2 The Modems Tab Screen of the Phone and Modem Options Screen.

Next, select the Diagnostics tab and click the **Query Modem** button, as shown in Fig. 49.3 below in which we show the action to be taken and the result of this action.

If under 'Response' it displays the word 'success' your modem is working fine.

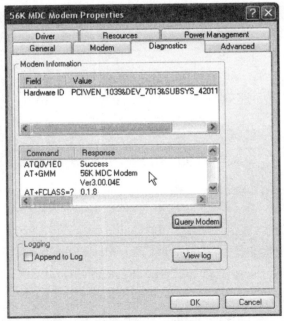

Fig. 49.3 Performing a Diagnostic Test on your Modem.

50

Controlling E-mail Sources

The Blocked Senders List

With Outlook Express there is a very easy way to prevent messages from a problem source ever disturbing you again. When you first receive a problem message, select it in the **Messages List** and action the **Message, Block Sender** menu command, as we did in the example in Fig. 50.1 below.

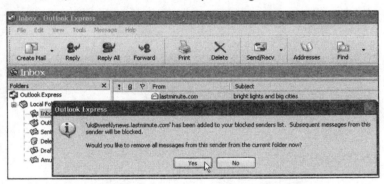

Fig. 50.1 Blocking Messages from a Single Source.

This can be a very powerful tool, but be careful not to block messages that you really would rather have received!

The **Message, Create Rule from Message** menu command is a quick way to start the **New Rule** process, as the details of the currently selected message are automatically placed in the New Mail Rule box for you, as shown in Fig. 50.2 overleaf.

People that send mass junk mailings often buy lists of e-mail addresses and once you are on a list you can be sure that your mailbox will never be empty again! With these tools at your disposal you should only ever receive 'junk mail' once from any particular source.

Fig. 50.2 Creating Message Rules, Box 1.

Using Message Rules

If you receive junk mail and you want to be in control, use the **Message Rules** menu option to filter your incoming messages. Unwanted ones can be placed in your **Deleted Items** folder straight away. It can also be useful for sorting incoming messages and automatically directing them to their correct folders.

To open this feature, which is shown in Fig. 50.3 on the next page, use the **Tools**, **Message Rules**, **Mail** menu command and select the criteria you want your incoming messages to be processed by.

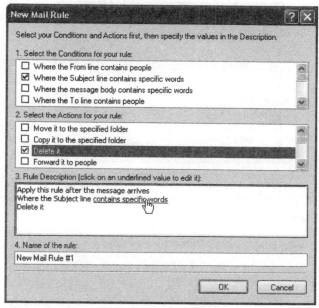

Fig. 50.3 Creating Message Rules, Box 2.

In the first box, shown in Fig. 50.3, you select the conditions for the new rule. In box 2 you control what actions are taken, and the new rule itself is automatically 'built' for you in box 3. If you use this feature much you will probably want to name each of your rules in box 4.

In Fig. 50.4, shown on the next page, we have set to intercept and delete messages which contain certain words in their Subject Lines. To complete the rule we clicked on the 'contains specific words' link and filled in the following dialogue box, clicking the **Add** button after each phrase.

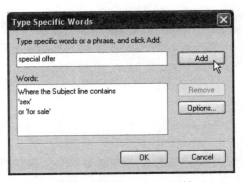

Fig. 50.4 Entering Words to Act Upon.

When finished clicking on **OK** twice opens the Message Rules dialogue box shown in Fig. 50.5 below.

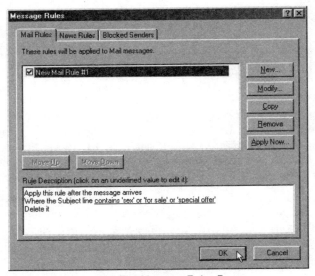

Fig. 50.5 The Message Rules Box.

In this box you can set multiple rules for incoming messages and control the sort priority for the list. The higher up a multiple list a condition is the higher will be its priority. If an incoming message matches more than one rule, then it is sorted according to the first rule it matches in your list.

Sending Video Clips via E-mail

Some digital cameras have the facility of recording short video clips of 15-30 seconds duration in audio video interleaved (**.avi**) format - it interleaves waveform audio and digital video. These can be viewed on your PC's Media Player, but can be rather large (2.5-4.5 MB) in size to send as an e-mail attachment to friends or relatives. Such files cannot be shrunk in the way scanned or digital camera pictures can, but there is a way of dealing with the problem.

To shrink such an audio video file, use *start*, **All Programs**, **Accessories**, and select the **Windows Movie Maker** option from the displayed cascade menu. The program is loaded and displays on your screen as shown in Fig. 51.1.

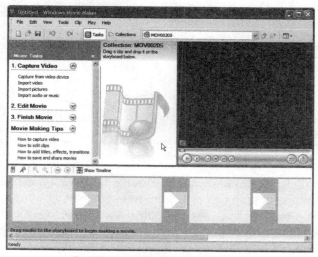

Fig. 51.1 The Movie Maker Screen.

Note: The various screens in this chapter might be different from yours, unless you have also installed Windows Service Pack 2. Nevertheless, this is not crucial, as the principle is the same.

Next, click the **Import Video** link under the **Movie Tasks** list to open the Import File dialogue box, then navigate to the video you want to send as an e-mail attachment, select it, and click the **Import** button. The screen will now look similar to the one in Fig. 51.2 below.

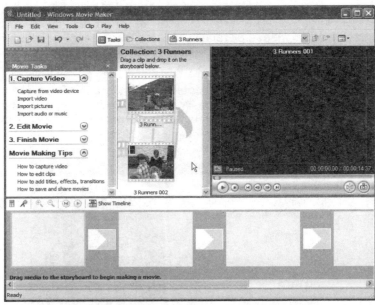

Fig. 51.2 Imported File into Movie Maker.

Next, drag the frames of your video to the Storyboard (the film strip at the bottom of the screen) to begin making a movie (you could use the **Edit Movie** option and look up the **Movie Making Tips** on the left pane if you want to add special effects, although you don't have to), and when ready, click the down-arrow against the **Finish Movie** entry to display available options, as shown in Fig. 51.3 on the next page.

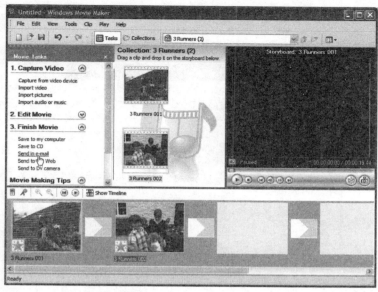

Fig. 51.3 Dragging the Clip onto the Movie Maker strip.

Next, click the **Send in e-mail** link pointed to in the screen above. This starts the Save Movie Wizard which shrinks the video clip, as shown in Fig. 51.4, ready for attaching it to an e-mail. If you have not installed SP2, save the shrunk video on your PC, then attach it to an e-mail in the usual way.

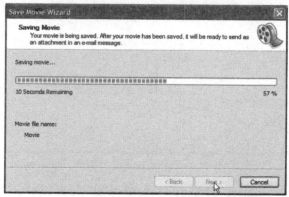

Fig. 51.4 The First Save Movie Wizard Screen.

The second Wizard screen, shown in Fig. 51.5, gives you the opportunity to either **Play ...** the shrunk version of the video, or **Save a copy ...** of it on your PC.

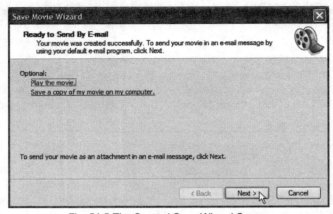

Fig. 51.5 The Second Save Wizard Screen.

To see the quality of the shrunk movie, you could choose the **Play the movie** option, otherwise click the **Next** button to open the **Outlook Express** e-mail box with the movie clip ready attached, as shown in Fig. 51.6 below. All you have to do is add a short message and send it on its way.

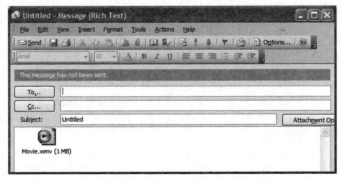

Fig. 51.6 The E-mail Window with a Movie Attachment.

Note that in this case, the video clip was shrunk from its original size of 6.74 MB to a mere 1 MB.

52

Creating a New User Account

If more than one person is to use your computer, then you may want to create an account for each person. Windows XP allows each user on your computer the means of customising their account to their own requirements. For example, they can customise their desktop, and they can customise the way windows display on screen.

Each user also benefits from having their own documents folder so their personal files are kept separate from those of other users, they have separate Internet settings, separate favourites and separate e-mail folders. Individual users can also password protect their accounts so everyone can feel safe in the knowledge that their individualised settings will not be changed by accident or intent. Most definitely, the computer administrators should password protect their accounts.

To create a new user account do the following:

* Log on as the administrator, then use the *start*, **Control Panel** menu command and double-click the **User Accounts** icon. In the displayed window, shown in Fig. 52.1 on the next page, click the **Create a new account** link under the **Pick a task** entry.

* In the displayed 'Name the new account' window, shown in Fig. 52.2 also on the next page, type in the name of the new account holder and click the **Next** button.

* If the person in question is too young, it might be a good idea to select **Limited** as the account type, on the next screen, and click the **Create Account** button.

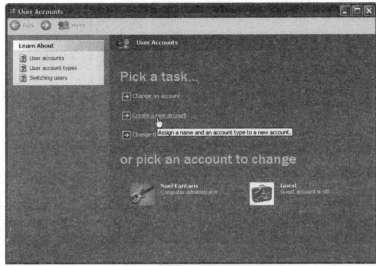

Fig. 52.1 Creating a New Account.

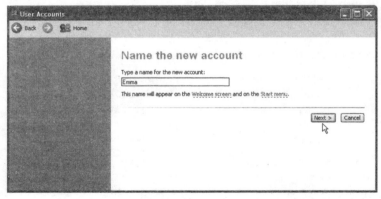

Fig. 52.2 Naming a New Account.

- On the next displayed window, shown in Fig. 52.3 on the next page, click on the newly created account under the **or pick an account to change**.

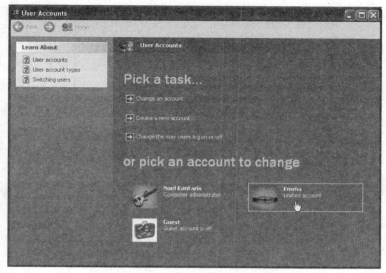

Fig. 52.3 Picking an Account to Change.

- On the displayed 'What do you want to change' window, shown in Fig. 52.4 below, click the **Change the picture** link (pointed to).

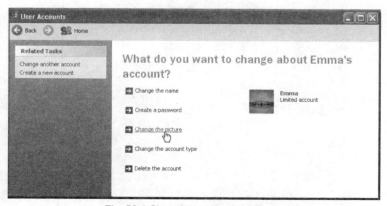

Fig. 52.4 Changing an Account Picture.

- In the displayed 'Pick a picture' window, shown in Fig. 52.5 below, select an appropriate picture and click the **Change Picture** button.

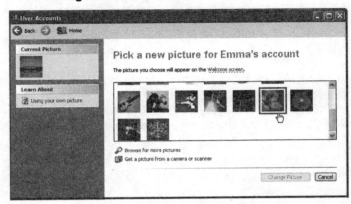

Fig. 52.5 Selecting an Account Picture.

- Next, the window of Fig. 52.4 is displayed once more where you can **Create a password** or click the **Home** Toolbar button to return to the 'Welcome screen' shown in Fig. 52.6 below.

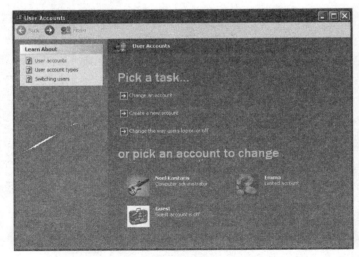

Fig. 52.6 The New Welcome Screen.

53

Switching User Accounts

In Windows XP there are two simple ways of switching users without having to restart the computer. However, if you are using Offline Files, you can only switch users by using the *start*, **Log Off** command and restarting the computer.

To use Fast Switching, you will have to disable the Offline Files option as follows: Log on as the administrator, then use the *start*, **Control Panel** menu command and in the displayed **User Accounts** screen, shown in Fig. 53.1, click the **Change the way users log on or off** link (pointed to) under the **Pick a task** entry.

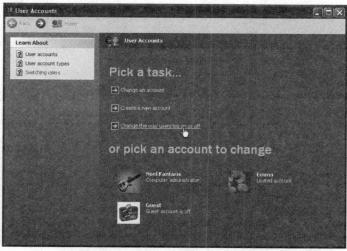

Fig. 53.1 Changing the Way Users Log On or Off.

On the displayed Offline Files Settings dialogue box, remove the check mark from the **Enable Offline Files** box, then click the **Apply** button followed by the **OK** button.

On the next window, shown in Fig. 53.2, select the **Use fast user switching** option and click the **Apply Options** button.

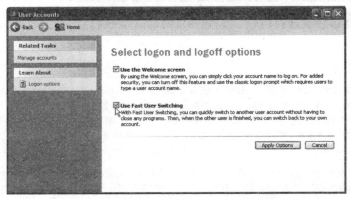

Fig. 53.2 Selecting Log On and Log Off Options.

Now using the *start*, **Log Off** command displays the box shown in Fig. 53.3 below. Clicking the **Switch User** option displays the Welcome screen shown in Fig. 53.4, showing all the users of the computer so that you can select one.

A faster method of getting to the Welcome screen is by pressing the **Windows logo** (⊞) and **L** keys together.

Fig. 53.3 The Log Off Windows box.

Fig. 53.4 The Windows Welcome Screen.

54

Activating the Guest Account

To provide limited computer access to guests to your home, who might require to look at and process their e-mail, for example, you need to activate the Guest account. To do so, log on as the computer administrator, and then on the User Accounts window click the Guest icon as shown in Fig. 54.1.

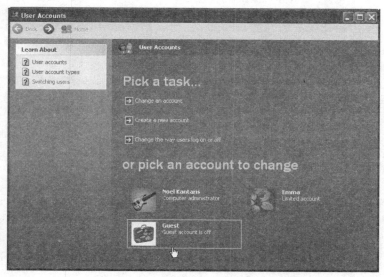

Fig. 54.1 Activating the Guest Account.

This opens the screen, shown in Fig. 54.2 on the next page, in which you click the **Turn On the Guest Account** button.

As with other users of this computer, a Guest account needs information about the person's e-mail provider, as discussed previously. An alternative option would be for the guest to use the Microsoft Hotmail facility, but to do so they must be online.

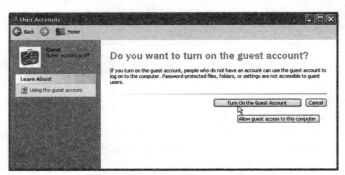

Fig. 54.2 Turning on the Guest Account.

Whichever e-mail facility you choose, as a Guest user you cannot connect to the Internet - they must get another user of this computer to first connect to the Internet before they can proceed. The same applies to disconnecting from the Internet after use.

To use Microsoft Hotmail, start Internet Explorer and type www.hotmail.com in the address box. This displays the screen in Fig. 54.3 in which you can either sign up for a free e-mail account (it must be activated within 10 days) or sign-in, if you already have an account established.

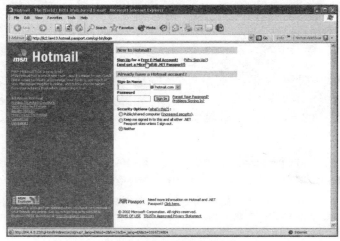

Fig. 54.3 The MSN Hotmail Sign-in Screen.

Increasing Computer Security

You can increase your computer's security by first disabling fast switching between users. To do so, log on as the computer's administrator, log off all other users by switching to their account and using the *start*, **Log Off** command, then do the following:

- Use the *start*, **Control Panel** menu command and click the **User Accounts** button. On the displayed screen click the **Change the way users log on or off** link.

- In the displayed 'Select logon and logoff options' screen, shown in Fig. 55.1, click the **Logon options** link under the **Learn About** entry on the left panel of the screen.

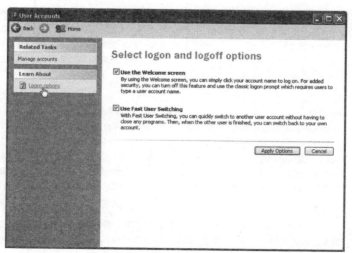

Fig. 55.1 Selecting Log On and Log Off Options.

- The displayed screen, shown in Fig. 55.2 below, contains information on what happens when either or both of the check marks in Fig. 55.1 are removed.

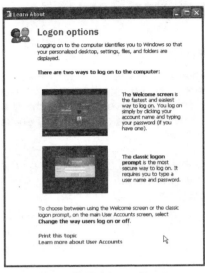

Fig. 55.2 The Learn About
Log-on Options Screen.

Obviously, disabling the Fast User Switching option adds a bit more security to the system, but it still retains the friendly way of logging in, as it allows you to click your name on the Welcome screen and type a password, if you have one, to log on.

However, if Fast User Switching is disabled, using the **Windows Logo** (🔲) and **L** keys together, locks the computer and only the administrator of the PC can unlock it. Also the Guest user is barred from browsing the Web or using any e-mail facility, because when a user who has access to the Internet logs off, the connection is shut down automatically.

If now, in addition to disabling the Fast User Switching option, you also disable the Welcome screen option, you increase security even more as you eliminate the possibility of a Trojan horse (a rogue program that collects information from your computer) disguising itself as a system log-on and retrieving user names and passwords that the writers of the Trojan horse can later use to break into your system when you are connected to the Internet.

In other words, increasing security decreases convenience of use of your computer, and vice versa. The choice is yours to make!

56

Paging File Security

When you try to run a program that is stored in a file, it is first copied into memory so that the CPU (Central Processing Unit) can execute the instructions it contains - it cannot be run directly from within the file it is stored in. Also data being processed by such a program must also reside in memory.

If a program uses up all the available memory (RAM) of your computer, portions of the program that are in memory, but have not been used recently are copied by Windows XP into a special file called **pagefile.sys**, known as the 'paging file'. This is the same as the 'swap file' in earlier versions of Windows.

Examination of this file with a disc editor can reveal to an unauthorised person the data you have been working with. If this is unacceptable for security reasons, then you can use a Windows option to wipe clean the paging file on shutting down the system. To do this, use the *start*, **Run** command, and in the displayed Run window type **gpedit.msc**, and click **OK**. This opens the Group Policy dialogue box shown in Fig. 56.1.

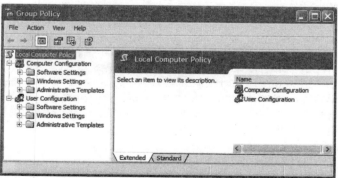

Fig. 56.1 The Group Policy Dialogue Box.

Next, expand the **Windows Settings** entry on the left pane, by clicking the **+** sign against its name, followed by the **Security Settings**, and the **Local Policies** entries. Finally, click the **Security Options** entry to display a large list on the right pane and scroll down to **Shutdown: Clear virtual memory pagefile** pointed to in Fig. 56.2.

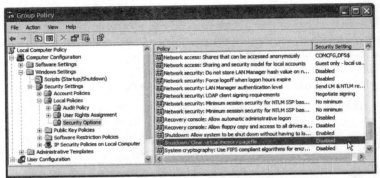

Fig. 56.2 The Security Options of the Group Policy Dialogue Box.

Double-clicking this entry, displays the screen in Fig. 56.3, in which you can change its **Security Setting** to **Enabled**.

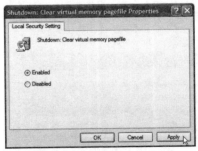

Fig. 56.3 The Pagefile Properties Box.

When this policy is enabled, it causes the system pagefile to be cleared when you shut down your PC. If you enable this security option, the hibernation file (**hiberfil.sys**) is also zeroed out when hibernation is disabled on a portable computer system.

57

Sharing Files & Folders

To share files and folders with other users of the same computer, first locate the files or folder you want to share (ours is a sub-folder in **My Documents** folder), select it and drag it to the **Shared Documents** link in **Other Places**. The file or folder will then be moved from its present position to within the **Shared Documents** folder.

Fig. 57.1 Drag-copying a Folder.

If you want to make a copy of the file or folder rather than move it, hold down the **Ctrl** key while dragging. You will be able to tell that the intended move will copy the file or folder by the display of the small plus (+) sign next to the mouse pointer, as shown in Fig. 57.1. When you release the mouse button a small dialogue box appears at the top-left of your screen, as shown here. To start the copying process, you must click the **Copy Here** entry which then displays the copying box shown in Fig. 57.2.

Fig. 57.2 The Copying Information Box.

To move or copy a file into the **Shared Documents** folder, select the file and click either the **Move this file** or the **Copy this file** link (Fig. 57.3). This opens the Move Items (or Copy Items) screen in which you select into which sub-folder in the **Shared Documents** folder you want to move or copy your selected file.

Fig. 57.3 The Internet Programs Screen.

It is a good idea to always move or copy an item into a meaningful sub-folder rather than moving or copying files into the main **Shared Documents** folder. If such a sub-folder does not exist, create it by using the **Make New Folder** button, while the **Shared Documents** folder is selected. The created folder will always be created within the folder you highlight in the Move or Copy dialogue box. To complete the Move or Copy command, select the sub-folder into which you want to place your file and click the **Move** (or **Copy**)

Fig. 57.4 The Move Items Screen.

button on the dialogue box in Fig. 57.4. As you can also see, the two folders, **Shared Music**, and **Shared Pictures** were created by Windows XP during installation for your convenience.

If you now use **My Computer** and open the **Shared Documents** folder, you will find the file you chose to share inside the newly created sub-folder.

58

FTP Files & Folders

You can use this option on the *start* menu to gain access to and get information on files and folders on other computers on a network or send files and folders to a Web site using FTP (File Transfer Protocol).

To begin the process, use the *start*, **My Network Places** menu command which displays the screen in Fig. 58.1 below.

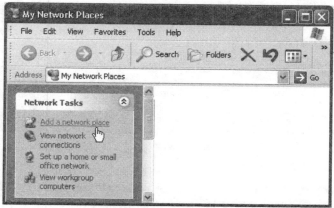

Fig. 58.1 The My Network Places Screen.

Next, click the **Add a network place** link under **Network Tasks** to start the **Add Network Place Wizard**, which helps you sign up for a service that offers online storage space, such as your Web site host.

On the second Wizard screen, click the **Next** button to display the third Wizard screen shown in Fig. 58.2 on the next page.

On this screen, type in the Internet or network address. Examples are displayed on the Wizard screen, as shown below, by clicking the appropriate link.

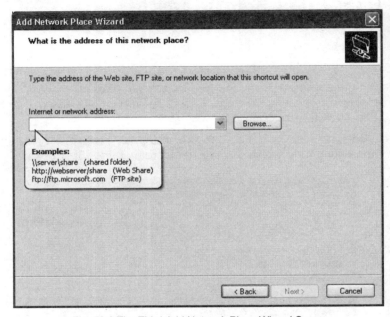

Fig. 58.2 The Third Add Network Place Wizard Screen.

What you type in the **Internet or network address** text box for uploading files using FTP should have been given to you by your Web site host. If it is a network address you are entering, then look at the examples above, or consult your network administrator.

On the fourth Wizard screen, you are asked whether you want to log on anonymously or provide a user name. To have full access to your Web site you should choose the latter option and provide the user name given to you by your Web site host, as shown in Fig. 58.3 on the next page

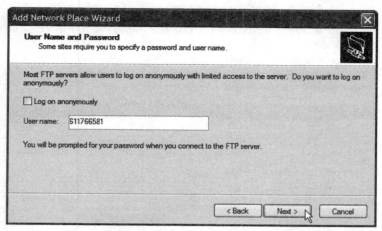

Fig. 58.3 The fourth Add Network Place Wizard Screen.

On the fifth Wizard screen, you are asked to provide a suitable
name for the connection which will appear in **My Network
Places**, and can be anything you like. After typing it in, click the
Next button to take you to the final Wizard screen, shown in
Fig. 58.4 below, in which you are asked to type in your
password.

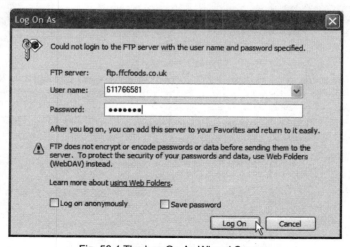

Fig. 58.4 The Log On As Wizard Screen.

In future, when you want to connect to the network place, use the *start*, **My Network Places** menu command and double-click the required entry. Alternatively, you could place a shortcut on your desktop by right-clicking the entry and selecting the **SendTo** option from the drop-down menu, as shown in Fig. 58.5.

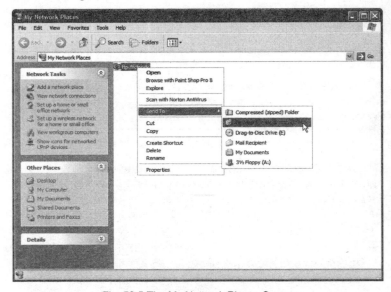

Fig. 58.5 The My Network Places Screen.

You could also drag the file to the desktop with the right button depressed, then on releasing the button, select the **Copy here** option from the displayed options.

59

Using the Command Prompt

If you are an experienced PC user, you may well prefer to do much of your specialised work by entering instructions in the Command window. Windows XP still lets you do this.

To display the Command Prompt window, click **start**, **All Programs, Accessories** and select the **Command** **Prompt** option from the cascade menu. This opens the window in Fig. 59.1 below.

Fig. 59.1 The Command Prompt Window.

If you use this method of working often, you might find it more convenient to place a shortcut to the **Command Prompt** icon on your desktop. To do this, right-click its entry on the cascade menu, then select **Send To, Desktop** from the displayed drop-down menu.

Note the absence of the toolbar on the above window from that of previous versions of Windows. However, most of the commands that were provided by such a toolbar can be carried out from the command menu.

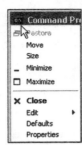

Fig. 59.2 The Command Shortcut Menu.

To illustrate this, let us change the appearance of the Command Prompt screen so that you can display, say, black lettering on a white background. To do this, click on the **Command** button (to be found at the upper left corner of the window) which displays the drop-down menu shown in Fig. 59.2 to the left. Next, select the **Properties** menu option which displays the dialogue box in Fig. 59.3.

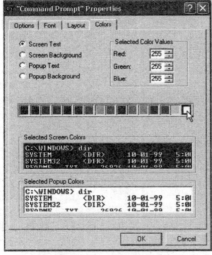

Fig. 59.3 The Properties Dialogue Box.

Here we show the Colors tab sheet in which we made the following selections:

Screen Text: Black
Screen Background: White
Popup Text: Blue
Popup Background: Grey.

In the Options tab sheet, you can select the Cursor Size, Display Options (window or full screen), Command History, and Edit Options. In the Font tab sheet you can select Font Size and Font Style. In the Layout tab sheet you can select Screen Buffer Size, Window Size, and Window Position. Pressing the **OK** button, displays an additional dialogue box, asking you to select between 'Apply properties to current window only', or 'Modify shortcut that started this window'. Choosing the latter will make your selections default for all sessions of the Command Prompt.

In Windows XP you use DOS commands in the Command Prompt window. To illustrate the point, type *dir* and press the **Enter** key. What is displayed is shown at the top half of the screen in Fig. 59.4 on the next page.

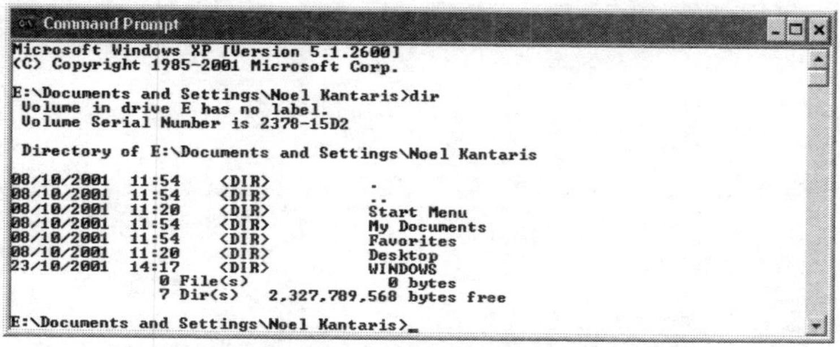

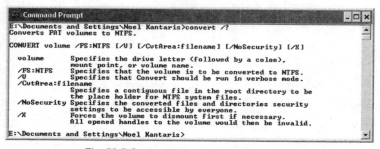

Fig. 59.4 The Structure of the Disc Holding Windows XP.

This, of course, is a typical DOS screen. To prove the point, type *dir /w* and press the **Enter** key. In fact, with Windows XP, the facility of using DOS commands in the Command Prompt window is mainly provided for backward compatibility and, therefore, if you want to adopt this method of working, we assume that you must be familiar with DOS commands, switches, filters, and batch files. Such files are most likely to be written by the System Administrator, to perhaps advertise to the network users, rules, events, or new packages.

All the available DOS commands are shown in Fig. 59.6, and can be displayed in the Command Prompt window by typing *help* followed by **Enter**. Information on individual commands can be displayed by either typing *help command_name*, or typing *command_name /?*. Either will produce an extensive list of command switches with explanation, as shown in Fig. 59.5.

Fig. 59.5 Getting Help with DOS Commands.

Fig. 59.6 The Available DOS Commands.

60

Assigning Keyboard Shortcuts to Programs

Sometimes it is much easier to assign a keyboard shortcut to a Windows application and start the program with the shortcut, than it is to navigate through the cascade *start* menu. As an example we will use the **Command Prompt** application, although one could apply the technique to any other program.

Normally, to start the **Command Prompt** program you will have to click the *start* button, then select **All Programs**, **Accessories** and select the **Command Prompt** option from the cascade menu, as shown in Fig. 60.1.

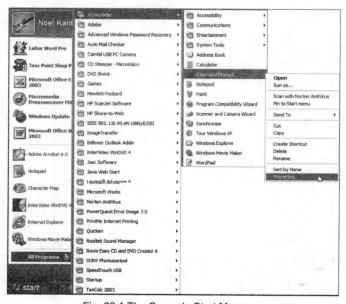

Fig. 60.1 The Cascade Start Menu.

If instead you right-click the **Command Prompt** entry, an additional quick menu is displayed as shown in Fig. 60.1. On this menu click the **Properties** option to open the dialogue box shown in Fig. 60.2 below.

Command Prompt Properties
General
Shortcut
Options
Font
Layout
Colors
Compatibility
Command Prompt
Target type: Application
Target location: system32
Target: %SystemRoot%\system32\cmd.exe
Start in: %HOMEDRIVE%%HOMEPATH%
Shortcut key: None
Run: Normal window
Comment: Performs text-based (command-line) functions.
Find Target...
Change Icon...
Advanced...
OK
Cancel
Apply

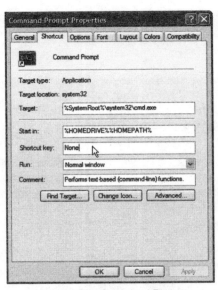

Fig. 60.2 The Command Prompt Properties Dialogue Box.

To see information relating to the **Shortcut key** pointed to in Fig. 60.2, click the ? button, then place the modified mouse pointer in the **Shortcut key** box and left-lick. This displays the information shown in Fig. 60.3.

Provides a space for you to type a keyboard shortcut that you press to start or switch to a program. Shortcut keys automatically include CTRL+ALT. Press the key you want to add to this combination. For example, to define the shortcut key combination CTRL+ALT+H, press H. You cannot use ESC, ENTER, TAB, the SPACEBAR, PRINT SCREEN, DELETE, or BACKSPACE.
No other program can use this key combination. If the shortcut key conflicts with an access key in a Windows-based program, the access key does not work. An access key is a letter or number that, when used in combination with the ALT key, carries out the same command as clicking the command with the mouse.

Fig. 60.3 Information Relating to the Shortcut Key of the Properties Dialogue Box.

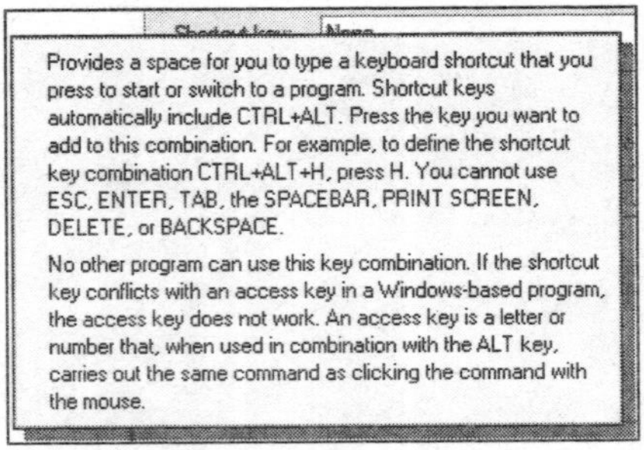

So, all you have to do is type one letter, say **P** for **Command Prompt**, the **Ctrl+Alt** key combination is then supplied by the program itself. Next, click **Apply**, followed by **OK**.

To test your newly created shortcut, press the **Ctrl+Alt** keys down and while holding them depressed, press the **P** key.

We further allocated the shortcuts **Ctrl+Alt+C** to **Character Map**, and **Ctrl+Alt+N** to **Notepad**. It does make activation of these programs much easier.

61

Running DOS Programs

With Windows XP, the easiest way to issue a single DOS command that involves running a program, is in the **Run**

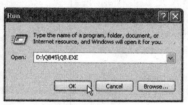

Fig. 61.1 The Run Window.

window, shown in Fig. 61.1, opened from the *start* menu. Its big advantage is that all previous commands are remembered. Clicking the down arrow, opens a small 'database' of your most used commands, including path and file names, etc. The command itself is actioned in a 'one off' Command Prompt window, as shown in Fig. 61.2 below.

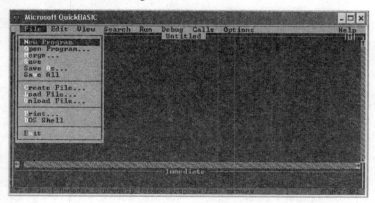

Fig. 61.2 Running a DOS Program in a Command Prompt Window.

To switch between full screen and a window, use the **Alt+Enter** key combination.

The MS-DOS Editor

Windows XP includes the **Edit** text editor, to be found in the **\WINDOWS\system32** subdirectory, as shown in Fig. 61.3.

Users of MS-DOS will find the editor very familiar, as the version provided in Windows XP is identical to that provided with earlier Windows versions. Improvements over much earlier versions of the program are:

Fig. 61.3 Running the Windows Edit.

- You can open up to nine files at the same time, split the screen between two files, and easily copy and paste information between them.

- You can open files as large as 4MB.

- You can open filenames and navigate through the directory structure just as you can in the rest of Windows.

The editor is opened, as one would expect from its name, by typing **Edit** at the Command Prompt, as shown in Fig. 61.4.

Fig. 61.4 The MS-DOS Text Editor.

The file opened in the editor's window above, is a **readme.txt** file in the background and a Cursor Movement Commands screen on the foreground, obtained by pressing the **F1** function key. To clear the screen, press the **Esc** key.

Copying Text from Old DOS Programs

You can copy text created in old DOS word processing programs and paste it in the latest and most favoured Windows application easily. To illustrate the process, we use below a letter we wrote more than five years ago, using our then loved Q&A word processor. You can follow the technique by using your own DOS word processed document.

First use the **Run** command to locate and load the DOS program, then open a document. Ours is shown in Fig. 61.5.

Fig. 61.5 Marking Text in a DOS Word Processing Program.

Next, click the **Command** button to open the drop-down menu and select the **Mark** option. This allows you to mark part or the whole of the document then use the **Edit, Copy** command to copy it onto the Windows clipboard, as shown in Fig. 61.6.

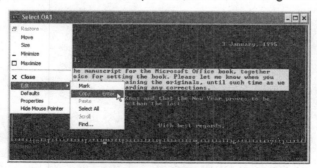

Fig. 61.6 Copying Text from a DOS Word Processing Program.

Finally, open your favourite Windows word processor and use its **Edit, Paste** command, to paste the contents of the clipboard into your new document. We used the WordPad application, as shown in Fig. 61.7 below.

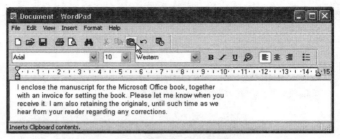

Fig. 61.7 Transferring Text into WordPad.

It is as easy as that. Perhaps this will prove the most useful and time-saving capability of the Command Prompt for most users.

62

Using Windows Startup Options

If Windows will not start for some reason, then turn your computer off and then back on again. As soon as any information starts being displayed on the screen, press the **F8** key. This displays the screen in Fig. 62.1 below.

```
Please select the operating system to start:

    Microsoft Windows XP Professional

Use the up and down arrow keys to move the highlight to your choice.
Press ENTER to choose.



For troubleshooting and advanced startup options for Windows, press F8.
```

Fig. 62.1 The First Startup Screen.

Here you can press **Enter** to start Microsoft Windows in the normal way, or press **F8** again to access the advanced startup options which displays the contents of Fig. 62.2 on the screen.

```
Windows Advanced Options Menu
Please select an option:

    Safe Mode
    Safe Mode with Networking
    Safe Mode with Command Prompt

    Enable Boot Logging
    Enable VGA Mode
    Last Known Good Configuration (your most recent settings that worked)
    Directory Services Restore Mode (Windows domain controllers only)
    Debugging Mode

    Start Windows Normally
    Reboot
    Return to OS Choices Menu

Use the up and down arrow keys to move the highlight to your choice.
```

Fig. 62.2 The Advanced Startup Options.

The various startup options allow the following capabilities:

Safe Mode

If your computer will not start, you might be able to start it in safe mode. In safe mode, Windows uses default settings (VGA monitor, Microsoft mouse driver (except serial mice), monitor, keyboard, mass storage, base video, and default system services, but no network connections.

This starting mode is used if your computer will not start after you install new software, which can be removed after starting your computer successfully in this mode. If a symptom does not reappear when you start in safe mode, you can eliminate the default settings and minimum device drivers as possible causes of the computer's inability to start.

If your computer does not start successfully using safe mode, you might need to use the Recovery Console feature to repair your system. This method will be discussed shortly.

Safe mode with Networking - Starts using only basic files and drivers, and network connections.

Safe mode with Command Prompt - Starts using only basic files and drivers. After logging on, the command prompt is displayed instead of the Windows graphical interface.

Enable Boot Logging - Starts while logging all the drivers and services that were loaded (or not loaded) by the system to a file. This file is called ntbtlog.txt and it is located in the %windir% directory. Safe Mode, Safe Mode with Networking, and Safe Mode with Command Prompt add to the boot log a list of all the drivers and services that are loaded. The boot log is useful in determining the exact cause of system startup problems.

Enable VGA Mode - Starts using the basic VGA driver. This mode is useful when you have installed a new driver for your video card that is causing Windows not to start properly. The basic video driver is always used when you start with any of the Safe Mode options.

Last Known Good Configuration

This startup option uses the Registry information and drivers that Windows saved at the last shutdown. Any changes made since the last successful startup will be lost. Use the Last Known Good Configuration option only in cases of incorrect configuration. It does not solve problems caused by corrupted or missing drivers or files.

Directory Service Restore Mode - This is for the server operating systems and is only used in restoring the SYSVOL directory and the Active Directory directory service on a domain controller.

Debugging Mode - Starts while sending debug information through a serial cable to another computer.

If you are using, or have used, Remote Installation Services to install Windows on your computer, you might see additional options related to restoring or recovering your system using Remote Install Services.

Using the Recovery Console

If Safe mode and other startup options do not work, you can consider using the Recovery Console. This method is recommended only if you are an advanced user who can use basic commands to identify and locate problem drivers and files. In addition, you must be an administrator and your Windows Setup disc must be current, that is, if you have updated your system to Windows Service Pack 1 or 2, then your Windows Setup CD must also contain this update, otherwise Windows will refuse to load an earlier version.

Using the Recovery Console, you can enable and disable services, format drives, read and write data on a local drive, and perform many other administrative tasks. The Recovery Console is particularly useful if you need to repair your system by copying a file from a floppy disc or CD-ROM to your hard drive, or if you need to reconfigure a service that is preventing your computer from starting properly.

There are two ways to start the Recovery Console: (a) You can run the Recovery Console from your Setup CD - see next chapter how to make your PC boot from the CD-ROM drive, or (b) you can install the Recovery Console on your computer to make it available in case you are unable to restart Windows. You can then select the Recovery Console option from the list of available operating systems on startup.

To install the Recovery Console as a startup option, you must be running Windows, then insert the Setup CD into the CD-ROM drive, click *start* and select **Run**. In the displayed Run dialogue box type the following where e: is the CD-ROM drive letter (yours might be different):

    e:\i386\winnt32.exe /cmdcons

then follow the instructions on the screen.

Now each time you start your computer, the screen in Fig. 62.3 is displayed.

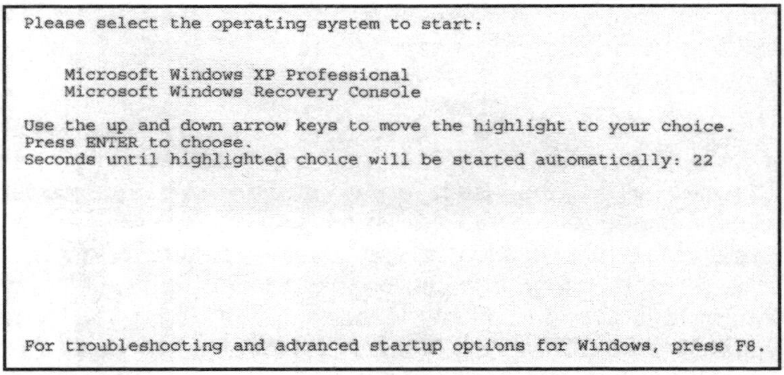

```
Please select the operating system to start:

    Microsoft Windows XP Professional
    Microsoft Windows Recovery Console

Use the up and down arrow keys to move the highlight to your choice.
Press ENTER to choose.
Seconds until highlighted choice will be started automatically: 22




For troubleshooting and advanced startup options for Windows, press F8.
```

Fig. 62.3 The Startup Options Screen.

Note: To run the Recovery Console, you must be logged on as an administrator or a member of the Administrators group in order to complete this procedure. If your computer is connected to a network, network policy settings may also prevent you from completing this procedure.

63

Making a PC Boot from the CD-ROM Drive

The latest computers are automatically configured to start from the CD-ROM drive, if the CD disc in it is a bootable disc. However, slightly older computers might not be so configured, in which case you will have to do it yourself.

To make your computer bootable from the CD-ROM drive, switch your computer off then on again, and while the boot program is checking the PC's memory, press the **Del** key (or whatever key you are told on your computer's display - it appears at the bottom left corner of the screen). This displays the first screen of the **CMOS SETUP UTILITY** program. The screen of one such program is shown in Fig. 63.1 below - yours might look quite different.

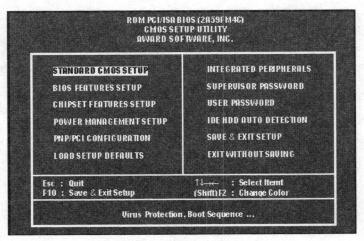

Fig. 63.1 The CMOS Setup Utility Screen.

From here, select the **BIOS FEATURES SETUP** option which displays the screen in Fig. 63.2. Other **CMOS UTILITY** programs might have a **Boot** option available on the first displayed screen of the utility, which when selected shows the boot sequence.

Continuing with the **CMOS SETUP UTILITY** of the slightly older PC, scroll down to the **Boot Sequence** option and select CDROM, C, A, by pressing the **Page Down** key (again the key might be different but it will be listed at the bottom of the screen) until this sequence appears on the screen.

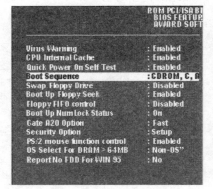

Finally, press the **Esc** key to return to the screen in Fig. 63.1, and select the

Fig. 63.2 Boot Sequence.

SAVE & EXIT SETUP option. The sequence for saving your changes and exiting the program might be different in your case, but it will be displayed on your utility's screen quite clearly.

Your PC should now restart automatically, and after the memory check, will boot from the CD-ROM drive provided you have inserted a bootable disc in it, such as the Windows Setup disc.

Index

Companion Discs

COMPANION DISCS are available for most computer books written by the same author(s) and published by BERNARD BABANI (publishing) LTD, as listed at the front of this book (except for those marked with an asterisk). These books contain many pages of file/program listings.

There is no Companion Disc for this book.

To obtain companion discs for other books, fill in the order form below, or a copy of it, enclose a cheque (payable to **P.R.M. Oliver**) or a postal order, and send it to the address given below. **Make sure you fill in your name and address** and specify the book number and title in your order.

Book No.	Book Name	Unit Price	Total Price
BP		£3.50	
BP		£3.50	
BP		£3.50	
Name		Sub-total	£.............
Address		P & P (@ 45p/disc)	£.............
		Total Due	£.............

Send to: P.R.M. Oliver, West Trevarth House, West Trevarth, Nr Redruth, Cornwall, TR16 5TJ

PLEASE NOTE

The author(s) are fully responsible for providing this Companion Disc service. The publishers of this book accept no responsibility for the supply, quality, or magnetic contents of the disc, or in respect of any damage, or injury that might be suffered or caused by its use.